Monetary Policy

DOUGLAS FISHER
Professor of Economics, Concordia University, Montreal

A HALSTED PRESS BOOK

JOHN WILEY & SONS
New York

First published in the United Kingdom 1976 by
The Macmillan Press Ltd

Published in the U.S.A. by
Halsted Press, a Division of
John Wiley & Sons, Inc.
New York

Printed in Great Britain

Library of Congress Cataloging in Publication Data

Fisher, Douglas, 1934–
　Monetary policy.

　"A Halsted Press book."
　Bibliography: p.
　1. Monetary policy.　I.　Title.
HG221.F524　1976　　　　332.4'6　　　　75-20330
ISBN 0 470-25996-5

Contents

1 Introduction

Practically everything which has been written in the vast macroeconomic literature has some relevance to the problems surrounding the formulation of an effective monetary policy. Perhaps the most obvious reason this is so is that a policy designed to influence the quantity or the price of the medium of exchange necessarily affects activity in every market because money is the one good which is traded in every market. Less mechanical reasons also exist. A broad scope is called for because fiscal and monetary policy, whether active or passive, are intertwined in a number of important ways: they work partly through the same channels; they are employed to reach the same objectives; and they are bound together by the fact that the note issue of the central bank confers 'earnings' on the central government, earnings which reduce the need to borrow or to tax. Furthermore, the central bank normally holds a substantial percentage of the national debt. But the most compelling reason for taking a broad view of the scope of monetary policy is that in order to conduct an effective policy, it turns out that the authorities must have as much information as they can possibly obtain about the workings of the economy. This information is generated both by their experiences and by the macroeconomic literature, particularly that which terminates in empirical tests. Let us elaborate on some of these issues before turning to more specific problems.

Following the development of the early macroeconomic models of the 1930s, presented, as they were, as a challenge to the conventional ideas of the role of the government, certain general objectives were enunciated in the 1940s in many countries, formally and otherwise, which have since been widely used as guidelines for policy. While the precise content of the phrase 'full employment' will normally be defined by some sort of political process, it is clear that adopting an official attitude toward, for example, the price level, the level of employment, the state of the balance of payments, and the growth rate of the economy, strongly suggests that a macro-economic policy will be formulated in which the values of these variables, however the variables are defined, will appear as the *objectives* to be attained. It also follows that the more precise we are willing to be about the desired values (or ranges) these variables should take on, the more easily we can construct econometric models to guide and inform us.

Rather naively, as it turns out, it was assumed in some quarters that not only was adequate knowledge of the economy readily available, but also that the simpler Keynesian (or, in some quarters, Classical) prescriptions were all that were needed to guide most economies toward their newly adopted objectives. In these early days, monetary policy was usually not thought of as an aid to the general objectives except in so far as easing the task of the Treasury in its various financial operations would contribute to general financial stability. Indeed, something like a 'rediscovery' of money occurred in the 1950s. This was the result of various events, but most notable was the effect of a persistent easy-money policy on the price level brought about by the Korean War. The result was the partial freeing of the monetary authorities from their assigned task of 'making' the market for government securities; this event took place in 1951 in both the United States and the United Kingdom. This interdependence between the central bank and the fiscal authorities, arising partly because the former markets the debt of the government, is a consistent feature of macroeconomic policy in all countries that practise it.[1]

[1]There is even more to the interdependence of the two than the overlap of objectives and the fact that an issue of currency reduces the need of the Treasury to resort to other means of finance. *Ceteris paribus*, an increase in the stock of money for policy reasons will raise the price of bonds (lower the interest rate) and permit an

8

It is not easy to overstate the dependence of the monetary authorities – to describe the persons whose job it is to carry out the instructions of the government (and the people) – on the state of the economic art. Every state of the policy problem requires that they have accurate information on what has happened in the economy and that they use this information as efficiently and correctly as the technology of economics permits. There are two related problems here: they need accurate and appropriate data – often quickly – and they need an effective and appropriate model of the economy; the latter must also include a description of the effects of the fiscal and monetary authorities themselves on the economy. Let us begin with a general description of the model.

An economic model serves several general purposes, sometimes simultaneously: it is used to describe a situation, *ceteris paribus*; it is used to generate predictions or forecasts; and it is used to help organise one's thoughts on economic problems. Again speaking quite generally, it is constructed so that certain entities are determined within the model (the endogenous variables); certain entities are taken as influential but are themselves determined outside the model (the exogenous variables); certain entities are taken as given (known) because they are historical facts (notably the lagged values of certain variables, often described as 'predetermined' variables); and certain variables are excluded because it is assumed they are irrelevant. The actual classification of variables into these categories is, to put it plainly, often as much a matter of convenience as it is of theoretical or practical insight.

In the first place, we must limit our study to those variables for which we have data. It is of little practical use to formulate a model requiring 'anticipated investment expenditure' by business corporations if such data is not collected by anyone. Yet it is also important to realise that, unless the crucial role of such an entity can be shown formally and persuasively, no one

---

expansion of income. The former will make it cheaper for the Treasury to float debt and the latter will increase its (income) tax revenues.

is likely to collect it.[1] A second limitation on our scope is the aforementioned 'state of the art'. If solutions are worked out for models in which the foreign-sector demand and supply schedules are treated as depending only on influences outside the economy, then a natural division between endogenous and exogenous variables is created for a very practical reason. Further, we have been speaking of both formal econometric models and the (often) informal perceptions of the actual policy-makers. Clearly a balance exists between the completeness of the model used, in the sense of endogenising as much as possible, and the ability to comprehend the results of conceptual experiments. The policy-maker has the additional constraint of having to communicate his recommendations (and his reasons for making them) to the layman.

Another important factor leading to the arbitrary classification of variables is the mythology surrounding certain popular systems of thought. At one time, for example, it was thought convenient to treat the money stock, however defined, as exogenously determined; indeed, both Keynesian and neoclassical economists did this, although for different reasons. We will argue below that this is not a useful position to take [24, 78]. The Keynesian view that 'money does not matter' justified a concentration on other sectors, particularly investment; this seems to have been refuted by experience. On the other hand, the often-used neoclassical assumption that the authorities can and do make the stock of money anything they want is on shaky grounds because there are both technical and economic factors complicating the relationship between the authorities' preferences and the final results. In any event, their assumption, coupled with the argument that 'money

[1]One of the important contributions of the *Radcliffe Report* [89] was to drive home to the U.K. government the need for more information on financial markets. In that document the requests for data were specific and forceful, and justified with respect to a theoretical perception of how the system worked. The latter has come under much criticism [9, 20, 46, 78], but the improved data which the monetary economist has had at his disposal since 1961 remains as an impressive monument to that document.

matters', has the effect of pushing much of the blame for many modern economic disturbances on to the monetary authorities or their counterparts, and even to suggest that we might be better off with rules of management, rather than with the discretionary actions of the authorities [37, 42]. But this is too simple a view of things, and there is actually overwhelming evidence in favour of treating the money stock as an endogenous variable, particularly, of course, in models of monetary policy.

Related both to the choice of which variables to include and which to exclude, as well as to the various doctrinal disputes, is the question of the level of aggregation of the model and its components. In the context of macroeconomics, the question of the appropriate aggregation is often also called the problem of the 'definition' of the concepts of the model [39, 67]. For example, we can 'define' the money stock to be the 'narrow' money stock, by which we mean that we will employ the sum (aggregate) of currency, plus demand (current-account) deposits. By and large, Keynesians, especially those who, like the Radcliffe Committee [89], believe in analysing the total stock of 'liquidity' in the economy, favour a broader definition of money than do those (usually neoclassically oriented economists) who favour the narrower 'medium of exchange' concept. But doctrinal issues aside, there is the fundamental question of how big the model is to be. Each new sub-division (disaggregation) of the most aggregate data (for example G.N.P.) requires new functional statements: if we are to work with a system which has a separation between currency and demand deposits, we must include equations describing how currency enters the system and, of course, we must describe the demand (function) for currency. Here, again, we run into the constraints imposed by our ability to model the more complicated situation as well as by the length and accuracy of the data series.

There are other 'aggregation' problems to deal with as well. Basically, in view of the fact that the data we observe are generated by individual decision-makers, any aggregation involves several strategic assumptions. The purpose of the aggregation, one might argue, is to provide a construct which, if it is an aggregation over goods, can be treated as a single good, or, if it is an aggregation over individual demand functions, can be treated as a single (individual) demand function, with all the properties of the single function of microeconomics. The most important of the conditions under which an aggregation over goods can be successful is that the price changes of the entities included in the composite should always be proportional [53, 83]. When we aggregate across individuals we require, roughly, that they all be alike, at least in their economic profiles. The cost of the aggregation, to weigh against the simplicity gained, is in the information suppressed. If the price changes between demand deposits and time deposits are not proportional in fact, then the aggregate may not behave itself in all uses and the predictions of our models, based on this 'broad' (M_2) aggregation, will tend to be less accurate. We probably will not know, as it turns out, especially if the price information is not available, but we will nevertheless have to pay the cost. Clearly these matters are worth some thought.

The purpose of this introduction has been to lay the ground-work for a broad definition of monetary policy. We have suggested that one of the most important problems which the monetary authorities face is the choice of a set of perceptions of the economy to use to guide them. This is a policy problem if only because their choice will critically influence the results they achieve, but it is also a policy problem because the ever-watchful legislator has a stake in the results. It was not without some careful thought that (former) President Nixon announced to a somewhat startled public that he was a Keynesian at last. The implication was that, twenty years behind the times, he would use the broad measures of fiscal policy if it became necessary. In other words, he judged that it was politically safe to take such measures. The fact that this announcement came after we were ten years past the onslaught of the 'monetarist revolution' gives one some food for thought. At any rate, the monetary authorities are often dominated by the executive in their operations, so such perceptions do have policy influences. We will see, beginning in Chapter 2 with a formal model, that all of the main elements of a monetary strategy – the choice of a model, the choice of objectives, and the choice of instruments to reach those objectives – is involved with policy issues that go beyond the simple economic analysis. But for now we turn to a discussion of procedures in the narrowest possible framework.

2 The Basic Model

INTRODUCTION

While Chapter 1 lays out a very broad context for the monetary-policy problem, and we will return to most of the issues raised there, an efficient place to begin our discussion is in a deterministic and static world in which the authorities have a firm and accurate picture of how the economy works, and are able to determine the quantity of money (or the interest rate) as they choose without any lags. In other words, let us assume the deterministic and static *ISLM* model popular in the literature since Keynes, in which the money stock is either an 'exogenous' or a 'policy-determined' variable [8].

THE COMMODITIES MARKET

Let us assume a consumption function as in equation (2.1), an investment function as in equation (2.2), and an equilibrium condition as in equation (2.3):[1]

$$\frac{C}{P} = f\left(\frac{Y}{P}, i\right), \qquad f_1 > 0, \quad f_2 < 0; \qquad (2.1)$$

$$\frac{I}{P} = g\left(\frac{Y}{P}, i\right), \qquad g_1 > 0, \quad g_2 < 0; \qquad (2.2)$$

$$\frac{Y}{P} = \frac{C}{P} + \frac{I}{P}, \qquad f_1 + g_1 < 1. \qquad (2.3)$$

[1]The notation f_1 defines the partial derivative of the function f with respect to its first argument Y/P.

All variables are in real terms (that is they are divided by the price level, P), and with the assumed values of the partial derivatives on the right-hand side of the page we would get a negatively sloped *IS* curve such as the one pictured in Figure 1. Thus, this system contains four 'real' variables (C/P, I/P, Y/P, i) in three equations, and the result of the application of the equilibrium condition (2.3) is a locus of pairs of values of i and Y/P which, with the appropriate restrictions, would look like the *IS* curve in Figure 1.

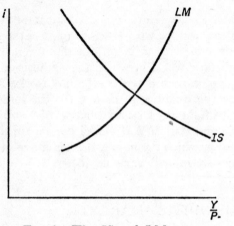

FIG. 1   The *IS* and *LM* curves

THE MONEY MARKET

Let us further assume a standard demand for money function, again in real terms, which is here exhibited as equation (2.4):

$$\frac{M}{P} = h\left(\frac{Y}{P}, i\right), \qquad h_1 > 0, \quad h_2 < 0. \qquad (2.4)$$

The effect of income on the demand for money is well-documented and unambiguously positive, but the magnitude of the interest-rate effect, representing the opportunity cost of holding money (and/or representing the speculative demand

16

for money) is not agreed upon by economists, although an enormous amount of work has been put into the problem. Nevertheless, the sign of the effect is usually thought to be negative (that is $h_2 < 0$).

If there is to be monetary policy in the model, then there has to be some mechanism whereby the authorities can influence the real variables in the system $(i, \Upsilon/P)$; these variables are the final variables in this discussion. We may suppose that the authorities determine the nominal quantity of money (M) through, say, open-market operations; this is not correct, as it turns out, and in Chapter 4 we will continue the discussion of the problem of achieving a money-stock target, but for now we will argue that such difficulties do not exist. The weakest model we could adopt here, and one already dismissed in Chapter 1, would argue that the authorities determine the money stock without regard to the values of the variables in the system, but this approach, equivalent to writing a money-supply function of $M = \bar{M}$, is deficient in two respects. In the first place it puts the responsibility for the determination of the values of the final variables in the economy solely on the shoulders of the authorities [25, 43]. In the second place it does not do justice to the fact that the authorities conduct a short-run policy, using the feedback from the system itself as a guide to their actual policy actions [25, 16, 95].

We may move somewhat closer to the requirements of real-world considerations if we argue that the authorities determine the nominal supply of money, but that they make this choice in response to changes in the interest rate or the price level. This relation appears as equation (2.5) and, it will be argued, this response will be stabilising on the interest rate. Thus

$$\bar{M} = j(i, P), \qquad j_1 > 0, \quad 1 > j_2 > 0. \qquad (2.5)$$

This formulation argues that a rise in interest rates will be interpreted by the authorities as a tightening of money markets and will provoke an increase in the money stock on their part. The condition on the second term, the price-level response, is assumed to be less than unitary in its effect to allow for the assumption of money illusion.

17

We may describe equilibrium in the money market and produce an *LM* curve to go along with the *IS* curve, by dividing both sides of equation (2.5) by the price level and solving for the various pairs of values of i and Y/P which equate equations (2.4) and (2.5). This exercise can be symbolised by equation (2.6) which can be written as

$$\frac{\bar{M}}{P} = \frac{M}{P}. \tag{26}$$

As one might expect, this exercise will produce a positively sloped *LM* curve under the assumptions just stated. But there is an important difference between the money-market and the commodity-market curves: the *LM* curve shifts with changes in the price level while the *IS* curve does not. In other words, the system of equations embodied in Figure 1 contains two equations and three unknowns $(Y/P, P, i)$ and, because of the existence of a monetary policy of the sort envisaged here, that is variations in the price level, a variable which we can take as indeterminate to this point, will influence the solution.

We can deduce the direction of this price effect on the *LM* curve as follows. The demand for money curve is in 'real' terms and carries the assumption, broadly, that money holders do not suffer from 'money illusion'. Thus, money holders perceive that an increase in their incomes and their money balances, sufficient to exactly match an increase in prices, will leave them just as well off as before these changes occur, and they act accordingly – the action in this case is to do nothing in 'real' terms. But the monetary authorities, if they are to affect the real variables in the system, must ignore changes in the value of money (to a certain extent) and stick to their objectives. Formally, there is money illusion assumed in equation (2.5), although we do not argue that this is 'perfect' illusion, or that it is in any sense 'irrational'; as things stand, money illusion in equation (2.4) would be described as irrational. The response given in equation (2.5) is a negative one: the real quantity of money offered by the authorities, at a given interest rate, declines as the price level rises. Thus the *LM* curve shifts to the left in response to a rise in prices and to the right (in a stimulatory direction) as the result of a fall in prices. The existence of a monetary policy of this sort (or of a nominal money stock not perfectly responsive to changes in the price level) produces this effect in the model. It remains to explain how the determination of prices might be achieved, assuming they are not actually determined exogenously.[1]

THE LABOUR MARKET

Let us assume an economy-wide production function as in equation (2.7), with two factors, Capital (K) and Labour (L), the former being fixed in quantity in order to achieve the assumption of a short-run model (that is $K = \bar{K}$). Thus

$$\frac{r}{P} = \phi(\bar{K}, L). \tag{2.7}$$

Let us suppose that the demand for labour, derived directly from equation (2.7), is a decreasing function of the real wage (W/P) – as described in equation (2.8) – and that the supply – as described in equation (2.9) – is an increasing function of the real wage: Thus

$$L^d = n\left(\frac{W}{P}\right), \qquad\qquad n_1 < 0; \tag{2.8}$$

$$L^s = k\left(\frac{W}{P}\right), \qquad\qquad k_1 > 0. \tag{2.9}$$

With a market-clearing equation, as in equation (2.10), the three equations (2.8), (2.9), and (2.10), are sufficient to

[1] A small country facing a set of world prices, or any country awash in a sea of foreign-exchange-created liquidity, could be described as one in which the price level is exogenously determined.

determine the three variables here, that is L^d, L^s, and W/P. Equation (2.10) is

$$L^d = L^s. \tag{2.10}$$

There is, therefore, no money illusion in the supply of labour function, and there are no rigid wages, so there is no particular reason to put unemployment (which cannot exist in this model anyway) in the authorities' policy function, represented in this model by equation (2.5). We may add another equation to link up equations (2.10) and (2.7); this can be written in the form of equation (2.11) as follows:

$$L = L^s. \tag{2.11}$$

With this condition, the set of five equations in this sector can determine five variables which are, as things stand, L^d, L^s, L, W/P, Y/P. The last variable, of course, was one of the three variables left over from the solution of the commodity and money markets so that, in effect, only two variables need to be explained by the *ISLM* equilibrium now. These could be i and P, and the model, therefore, is complete, with 11 equations and 11 unknowns (Y, P, M, $\bar{M}$, i, C, I, W, L^d, L^s, and L).

A GRAPHICAL SOLUTION OF THE SYSTEM

We may illustrate the situation, and show how the price level is determined, with reference to Figure 2. Here we see that since the labour market does not contain the interest rate, it is presented in the *ISLM* space (or i, Y/P space) as a vertical line. We may start, then, by assuming that the labour market is in equilibrium at a level of employment we can term the 'full-employment level'; accordingly, the real income which is fed into Figure 2 by means of equation (2.7) can be termed the 'full-employment income'. It is represented here by $(Y/P)_f$.

Suppose, then, that the *ISLM* equality for the economy was, for some reason, at point $\bar{a}$. This situation could have been

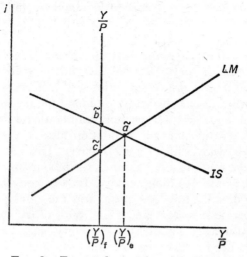

Fig. 2   Excess demand and inflation

brought about by a general increase in demand (a rightward shift of the *IS* curve), an increase in the supply of money (a rightward shift of the *LM* curve) or, of course, because of a leftward shift of the full-employment curve. Whatever its cause, it is a situation which we normally refer to as 'excess demand'. In other words, the economy, with present resources $(\bar{K}, L)$ can only produce real income up to the level of $(Y/P)_f$, but the sum of investment and consumption demand is at the larger total denoted by $(Y/P)_e$. When there is a condition of excess demand of this sort, prices will rise; as they rise, by our previous argument, the *LM* curve shifts to the left. A resting point, and one in which the price level is stable (but higher) is at point $\tilde{b}$ where equilibrium is assumed to exist in all markets.

That this is a model with viable monetary policy in it could easily be disguised by the formality of the exercise just conducted. The authorities here follow the practice of stabilising the capital markets rather than that of stabilising the price level, but it is a kind of monetary policy nevertheless. In terms of what they do with the money stock, then, it should be emphasised that, in going from point $\tilde{a}$ to point $\tilde{b}$, the interest rate has

21

risen producing an accommodating increase in the nominal money stock (by means of equation (2.5)). This 'accommodation' is also widely referred to as *validation* [9, 19]. Thus, if the economy arrived at point $\tilde{a}$ as the result of an increase in demand (demand-pull inflation) then this pressure was validated by the application of equation (2.5). That is, there is a positive association between the nominal money stock and the price level which is quite possibly unintentional, but is of the 'reverse' causation nature. Validation also occurs here when there is a leftward shift of the Y/P curve. This last could come about as the result of a reduction in the labour-supply function, perhaps because of union activity. In this case, the price rise might be described as 'cost push' and the validation is again non-deliberate in so far as it is the result of trying to stabilise the capital market. Finally, the monetary base of the economy could expand, for example because of a balance-of-payments surplus, producing a rightward shift of the LM curve; again the validation is incidental to the main role of the authorities, at least in so far as equation (2.5) describes this role.

In all of these cases there is a strong association between money and prices, and this, quite possibly, accounts for the association one observes over long runs of data for the developed countries. As things stand here, the authorities have no control over prices, and if they shift from a pursuit of interest-rate stability to one of price-level stability, they will have to abandon the capital markets. The interest rate, then, will be determined by the 'real' part of the economy. We see, therefore, where fiscal policy could enter, for one could avoid the price-level change which takes us from $\tilde{a}$ to $\tilde{b}$ by reducing government spending or increasing taxes and thereby shifting the IS curve (suitably defined to include the government) down to the left. The main point, thus, is that to achieve both interest-rate and price stability in a world of continuing and unpredictable changes in domestic and foreign spending, where the sources of the trouble are hard to detect, both fiscal and monetary policy are necessary. This point generalises to the case where there are many specific objectives.

EXPECTATIONS AND MONETARY POLICY

Using an interest-rate target, as the previous model suggested, is an appropriate approach in a world as simple as that just modelled, but in a world in which the pressures are such as to produce wide variations in the rate of inflation, this will not do. Indeed, it is quite possible that this kind of 'defensive' monetary-policy strategy will exacerbate an already poor situation. We will consider one case of that here, that of the validation of inflationary expectations. Again we employ the *ISLM* model.

If the inflation rate is variable, then whenever individuals engage in contracts for which the contract is one denoted in nominal (money) terms, their expectations of what is going to happen to prices become part of the deal. That is, a lender of money, expecting to receive later a money payment reduced in purchasing power by the rate of inflation, will mark up his interest charge in proportion to what he expects to lose thereby. The borrower, who expects to pay back in depreciated money, will be willing (if rational) to pay a higher rate, and if both lender and borrower agree on the inflation rate (and on the underlying 'real' interest rate), then a bargain will be struck such that equation (2.12) holds, that is

$$i = r + (\Delta P/P)^e. \tag{2.12}$$

The variable $(\Delta P/P)^e$ represents the expected inflation rate and r is the underlying 'real' rate; i, consequently, is the money rate of interest which we can actually observe ruling in financial markets.

In so far as the *IS* curve is concerned, it seems reasonable to argue that all calculations between present and future consumption, and on how much to invest, will be on the basis of r, the real rate of interest. In other words, consumers as a whole may well expect their incomes to rise as much as the prices of commodities, and businessmen, similarly, may well expect to receive their share of the inflated proceeds of econo-

23

mic activity. Thus we should rewrite equations (2.1) and (2.2) in real interest-rate terms, as described in equations (2.13) and (2.14), that is

$$\frac{C}{P} = f\left(\frac{Y}{P}, r\right), \tag{2.13}$$

and

$$\frac{I}{P} = g\left(\frac{Y}{P}, r\right). \tag{2.14}$$

If we continue to solve our system in terms of i and (Y/P), as in Figure 2, then the effect is that a shift in expectations will shift the IS curve in the i dimension employed there. We may see the direction of this effect by noting, in equation (2.12), that a rise in the rate of inflation expected, given i, will reduce the real rate of interest investors (or consumers) expect to have to pay on borrowed funds. This fact will stimulate investment. Similarly, at a lower real rate of return, the incentive to save would be less (probably), implying a rise in spending on consumer goods (in the present). Both of these forces would produce a rise in total spending and a rightward shift in the IS curve, as pictured in Figure 3.

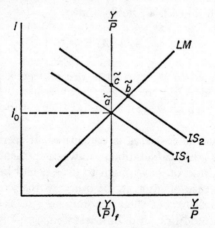

Fig. 3   Monetary policy and inflationary expectations

The monetary sector in this revised model would continue to be written in terms of the nominal interest rate, for inflationary expectations ought to be included in calculations of demands and supplies of assets and liabilities denoted in money terms (as we argued at the beginning of this section). Thus the 'movement' from point $\tilde{a}$ to point $\breve{b}$ would occur because of the rise in nominal interest rates as expectations of rising prices directly affected lending and borrowing activities in the capital markets. (These relationships can be seen in equations (2.4), (2.5), and (2.6).)

The situation, then, is that the economy has been driven to point $\breve{b}$, a position of excess demand, by the rightward shift in the *IS* curve, itself a result of the inflationary expectations. This excess demand, as before, would tend to produce rising prices. Validation, then, would shift the *LM* curve, as before, possibly until point $\tilde{c}$ is reached. What is different about this situation is that the causes are in a manner of speaking 'unreal' in that only an expected inflation occurred to upset things. The validation, one might say, took the form of actually producing the inflation which was only an expected inflation until the authorities went into action. This case is clearly a worrying one in that perfectly reasonable rules of thumb seem to get us into serious trouble. Furthermore, and this is what really worries some monetarists [8, 42], it is possible that the inflation we incur in our movement from $\breve{b}$ to $\tilde{c}$ will reinforce the worst fears of those who expected inflation in the first place, producing further expectations of an inflation, which might again be validated. The process could go on for a long time (as long as the rules of the game are not changed) and even accelerate, if continued bad news produces over-reaction in some sectors. Worrisome, as well, is the possibility that random events can trigger such reactions. The potential impact of the massive oil revenues of the Arab countries on the monetary bases of the oil-importing countries is one such case in point: a rise in 'caused' inflation could induce expected inflation which, if validated, could lead to the whole thing exploding.

A cheerful note could be sounded here, of course, in that

the authorities could always abandon the interest-rate policy and refuse to permit the validation of inflationary expectations (or any other cause). But, as long as we are letting realism creep in, we should also note that we actually live in a world of 'stagflation'. That is the case when point $\tilde{a}$ is to the left of the (Y/P) line, so that the process just described leads to rising unemployment and rising prices (possibly accelerating) occurring at the same time. We will return to some of these issues in the following chapters, but for now we will turn in Chapter 3 to some more of the problems of the implementation of policy.

3 Technical Problems in the Conduct of Monetary Policy

INTRODUCTION

In Chapters 1 and 2 we generally took the line that the monetary authorities can determine the money stock and that they do so for definite reasons, whatever they might be. The facts do not correspond to this simple-minded view of things and it is now time to elaborate on some of the problems which arise in the conduct of an actual monetary policy. First, it is clear that the objectives of monetary policy – defined as values or ranges of values of certain key variables (for example unemployment) or, loosely, the variables themselves – are (a) not always definite, (b) frequently changed, (c) sometimes inappropriate, and (d) generally unachievable all at once. Secondly, it turns out that the authorities have problems with the instruments (for example open-market operations) in their policy arsenal: they are sometimes clumsy, often inappropriate, occasionally 'noisy', and, too often, inefficient in their operation. Thirdly, the authorities possess neither a perfect model of the economy nor perfectly accurate data to feed into it if they had it anyway, with the result that they must grope their way to, at best, a short-run solution to their problems. In this groping process they may use intermediate targets which are more visible (for example the level of 'free reserves') and intermediate indicators of how they are doing; the money stock may serve well in the latter capacity.

THE OBJECTIVES

The actual working objectives of the monetary authorities of a nation are obviously very specific to the environment in which they appear in both a temporary and a geographical sense. While we can easily exaggerate this essentially institutional determination, it is clearly important to put oneself into the specific framework in which policy is conducted in order to gain a full appreciation of the problems. For example, the discussion in Chapter 2 is more appropriate for a developed post-1945 economy, in which the authorities have been instructed to monitor certain variables – such as the level of employment – than to a less-developed country. It also, presumably, better describes a modern economy than the economies of earlier times, for, under the circumstances then, monetary policy, as we know it, only rarely existed, and never for long periods of time.

The objectives are changed, of course, from time to time as a nation's collective values change and as the general perception as to what is feasible changes. In the heyday of the 'Keynesian Revolution' it was felt that the means were at hand to directly affect the economy swiftly and powerfully; the stated objectives then tended to be somewhat firm ('for example no more than one per cent inflation') and, by modern standards hard to hit. But with a long series of disappointments in the policy area in most Western economies, our confidence in the efficiency of monetary and fiscal policy has ebbed somewhat, particularly for 'fine-tuning' operations, and our objectives, reflecting what we now feel to be feasible, have become considerably more vague and are pitched at more easily achieved levels [92]. Let us consider some of the specific problems which arise in trying to formulate more precise objectives.

The first problem which arises is essentially in the enumeration of objectives and in the delineation of 'intermediate' from 'final' objectives. Usually one can find some exact reference in the literature to the following general objectives, although the specific qualifying words change with the circumstances [23, 89]. They are 'price stability', full employment' 'satisfactory balance of payments', and 'rapid rate of growth'. To this one might add a 'stable capital market'.

Consider, first, the price level. If prices are growing steadily at, say, two per cent a year, then an economy can accommodate itself to the situation by simple escalator clauses or by constructing pay scales that reflect the inflation rate. Further, since interest rates will tend to reflect the expected rate of inflation, with a steady two per cent inflation, expected inflation will tend to equal actual inflation, and money interest rates will simply be marked up by two per cent, so that capital markets will not be unduly disturbed (but see the discussion in Chapter 4 for some complications). Thus the frustration of expectations and some of the undesirable distributional effects of a variable inflation rate will not occur to concern the authorities. These remarks establish that the appropriate variable to measure price effects is the rate of change of prices and it is mainly important in causing expectations to be frustrated or in causing spending and investment plans to be constructed with an eye to an escape if things turn out badly. But, as it turns out, in a number of cases the authorities actually seem to monitor the *level* of prices rather than the rate of change [89, 32, 33, 86]. The best answers one can give, without further study, are that either (a) the true long-run objective of the authorities in such cases is the level of prices, or (b) the authorities do not have an adequate model of price-level dynamics and thus use the static goal as a proxy [80]. We see again the possible dependence the authorities have on the state of knowledge.

While it may be appropriate to watch the price level rather than the rate of inflation, when it comes to the 'full-employment' objective, the level of the variable is what matters. The question which first arises, however, concerns whether or not 'unemployment' as a percentage of the labour force is the appropriate objective variable. For one thing, the monetary authorities themselves may be instructed to watch the level of employment rather than the rate of unemployment, leaving the latter to social rather than macroeconomic policy. Secondly, the rate of unemployment will not reflect (a) the under-employment which results from workers taking jobs which do not fully utilise (and pay for) their skills or (b) the fact that the size of the labour force itself will vary with the state of the economy. In hard times, for example, workers retire early; further, when jobs are plentiful workers may join the ranks of the unemployed in order to conduct a more efficient job search.

But of even more consequence is an idea put forward recently by Milton Friedman [44] that adoption of a particular rate of unemployment in defiance of the rate which is *natural* for the economy (as a result of supply and demand working themselves out) could lead to the authorities actually destabilising the economy. Suppose, for example, that the natural rate of unemployment were to rise because of an influx of foreign workers or on account of the entry of a significant number of women into the work force. The authorities would observe a rise in unemployment and increase the money supply, as per their operating instructions. In the short run, especially, the price level would tend to increase as the actual rate of unemployment is driven – by the monetary authorities – below the natural rate toward the desired rate of the authorities. Real wages would fall and money wages would rise; the former would increase the demand for workers, the latter would increase the supply (if workers suffered from money illusion). But eventually, as the price inflation becomes accepted, workers' contracts would reflect (build-in) the inflation, and unemployment would reappear. The authorities, this time, would have to step up the rate of production of the money stock, leading to an acceleration of the rate of inflation; this process would not stop until the authorities changed their operating procedures. This view, to which we will return in the appendix to Chapter 4, has been dubbed the 'accelerationist hypothesis'; it relies on the official adoption of a goal which, to say the least, may be ill-advised. One should note, before going on, that trying to tie the actual rate of unemployment to the natural rate is not an obvious solution to the problem, since the latter is not easy to measure – being essentially unobservable – as well as constantly on the move.

30

With respect to the balance of payments, one has to question whether or not the needs of society here are insatiable. Furthermore, it is necessary to be clear as to what it is that is supposed to be 'satisfactory' here. The total of gold, convertible currencies, net International Monetary Fund balances and unused Special Drawing Rights is a widely accepted total, but in recent years it has become realised that since 'convertible currencies' are anything that central banks actually hold by agreement with other central banks, this total is subject to negotiations between central banks rather than necessarily to any direct economic processes as such. We note, in particular, the recent astronomical rise of U.S. dollars held by many other central banks around the world. It is very difficult to capture the political aspects suggested here; at any rate, we will return to this problem in our discussion in Chapter 6.

In recent years a voluminous literature, much of it in a popular form, has considered the validity of having a growth objective. In all likelihood, the authorities of most countries have not used monetary policy to help achieve a desired rate of growth of the economy [28, 33, 90]; but even so nothing is more widely debated these days, and one suspects that if social trade-offs between the rate of growth and the depletion of resources are eventually established, then because of the clear trade-offs between the rate of growth and the objectives already discussed in this chapter, a broader set of objectives will become relevant in the discussion of monetary policy. The reader interested in a preview of some of the issues which arise would do well to consult the collection of readings edited by N. Kaldor [60].

There is one final aspect of the objectives problem which arises mainly because the link between the instruments and the final variables is quite possibly long and unstable over time. Friedman [40], for example, has argued that the link between the money stock and the price level may reasonably be expected to be anywhere between six and eighteen months, on the basis of his reading of the U.S. experience, and that a monetary policy is hazardous indeed if stability of the price level in the face of exogenous shocks is desired [38, 40]. One result has been that the authorities have sought to redefine their goals in terms of the intermediate variables, such as the stability of the interest rate over time or, even, the 'maintenance of orderly conditions in the government-securities market', rather than in terms of the final variables. Such policies, also sometimes referred to as 'tone and feel' policies, have been popular in both the United States and the United Kingdom, and can be justified formally and reasonably if stability of a segment of the capital market can be linked to stability of the final variables. This seems unlikely, and some writers have pleaded for more 'objective' objectives [7, 47].

THE INSTRUMENTS

What has not been recognised so far in our discussion is that considerable 'disutility' attaches to the use of a policy instrument at all, and that this disutility is in direct contrast to the gains the authorities might make by achieving some of the explicit goals just described. We detect here a general bias toward inaction, and we should recognise that a desirable state of affairs for the authorities might be one in which the goal variables nicely offset each other (a lot of inflation associated with a rapid growth rate) so that no policy action is required. The gist of this new point is that the instruments themselves might become objectives (in a sense) for some of the reasons which follow.

At a fairly simple level, it could be argued that the instruments belong in any perception of the social-utility function because any use of them is upsetting. More specifically, their use has been conjectured to be disturbing to the financial community: it is alleged that U.S. commercial bankers do not like changes in reserve requirements because these force them to make large and expensive adjustments in their portfolios [63]. Then, too, there are explicit costs involved in changing the instruments. For example, open-market operations often involve brokerage fees, and changes in tax rates involve starting up the fiscal machinery, with an expensive use of precious legislative time involved. Another popular reason is that controls of this sort interfere with the domestic allocation of resources and that the authorities can always expect to come under pressure depending on whose resource is being reallocated. For example, the general application of monetary policy in the 1960s in the United States seemed to produce acute difficulties in the housing industry and, not accidentally, an interruption in the growth of home ownership, a consequence of considerable social implication. Indeed, U.S. citizens have not forgotten this experience, which is now deemed to be one of the recurring costs of 'tight money'. In the United Kingdom the application of hire-purchase controls deals blows to the purchase of consumer durables; in this case there is evidence that there is considerable activity in this sector just before or just after a new budget is announced. Finally, it is possible that the limelight of publicity surrounding policy changes is considered directly undesirable to the authorities themselves, or the government they are serving; this, too, would suggest considering the instruments themselves as 'objective' variables. Some such consideration as this might have led, in the new 'competition and credit control' policy recently adopted by the U.K. government [10], to the ending of the formal and discrete changes in Bank Rate as a policy variable in favour of more continuous changes in the Bank of England's discount rate.

TARGETS AND INDICATORS [14, 15, 16, 34, 95]

The discussion so far has actually evaded what might be the central question in monetary policy: in a world in which the authorities have imperfect knowledge of the causation and the timing of causation with regard to the determination of the final variables in the system, what operating rules and provisional techniques ought they to employ to instruct and guide them. They need, in short, to know what effect they are having as a result of past changes in instruments, and what other effects are going on simultaneously. It is easily recognisable that what is involved here is basic to the problem, since it

33

involves living in the real world; while there are other issues, involving improvements in the basic design of models to include 'stochastic' elements, here we will discuss the division of the intermediate financial variables through which monetary influences flow into two sets of variables: a set of targets which can be hit by the policy instruments and a set of indicators which measure the effect of the policy actions on the final variables.

To begin with, we should emphasise that the problem arises in the first instance because, as we have noted, the authorities possess only limited information about the structure and workings of the economy. In other words, they need to know about the general shape of the structure of the economy, the impact of exogenous forces, and the size, significance, and stability of the parameters of the system in order to allow them to follow the simple-minded approach implicit in the model presented in Chapter 2. The monetary authorities must make do with the information which they possess; what they possess is a series of half-verified hypotheses (for example, that the demand for money is a stable function of a few key variables), some often inconsistent forecasts from econometric models and from other less formal sources, and a great deal of practical information on how financial markets function. Since their information on financial markets is likely to be the best of this lot, it is small wonder that an alternative to what we might now describe as a 'full-information' monetary policy is adopted. This alternative takes the form of selecting certain financial variables to be targets and certain others to be indicators, as already suggested. The details of this choice depend on the information available, on certain logical restrictions, and, of course, on the authorities' perceptions of, and prejudices about, the economic system.

Before considering the basis for this choice, let us consider some definitional problems. First, let us note that the word 'target' is defined here to mean the value of the intermediate financial variable that is under the direct and unambiguous influence of one or more of the instruments. This is emphasised now because there is a tendency to define words like 'target' with considerable model specificity; for example, one hears of interest-rate 'targets', money-stock 'targets', and even price-level or growth 'targets'. In this study, we are referring to the final variables which the authorities are instructed to aim at as 'goal' or 'objective' variables, rather than targets. We note, however, that one of the goals, the authorities' assumption of responsibility for maintaining orderly financial markets and, in particular, for seeing that Treasury operations are not accompanied by unduly large changes in interest rates or in private, corporate, and bank portfolios, should really be referred to as an 'intermediate goal' since stability of financial markets is not usually thought of as an end in itself, at least by a large part of the electorate.

One might at first glance think, in view of the fact that the authorities possess full information about their own instrument settings, that they possess sufficient information to measure the impact of policy adjustments on the goal variables, but for a number of reasons, this is not so. One major difficulty is that all sorts of lags exist in the response of the system to various impulses; and not only do the lags vary from cause to cause but also they vary from period to period, making it most difficult to disentangle the effects of known influences, let alone the effects of the unknown. Even more serious, perhaps, is the influence of the unknown: exogenous influences affect every aspect of a nation's economic life. In particular, exogenous factors are known to influence both the goal variables and the intermediate financial variables. Take two simple examples: it is a very large country indeed which can assert that world prices do not affect domestic prices (an objective variable) and, similarly, the dependence of domestic interest rates on world interest rates (an intermediate variable) is generally thought to be pervasive. Worse, there are many other exogenous influences to consider for, as noted above, the word 'exogenous' in the economist's parlance refers not only to influences from outside the economy, but also to influences from outside his particular model. Thus, for the monetary authorities, the list of what is essentially exogenous – and therefore disturbing to the line of causation from instrument to goal variable – depends on how much they know about the nature and workings of the economic system. That, clearly, is not sufficient to enable them to discern the impact of their instruments on the final variables.

Our criteria for target variables are essentially two in number: that they

(T1) be quickly and firmly influenced by the instruments at hand, and that they be

(T2) readily and accurately measurable.

Thus, we require that the target be influenced by the instruments and that the variable be a relatively measurable one; this latter condition rules out such variables as the 'tone and feel' of the market, not because it isn't visible, but because it is an unquantifiable concept, it is subject to the shortcoming that two different observers will generally provide two different estimates of its direction [7, 47, 66]. Immediately one sees why interest rates are such a popular target variable; they are readily observable on a daily basis and they seem to respond directly to monetary pressures. Indeed, as the work described in the next two chapters suggests, they may even over-react, depending on the nature of the policy.

The indicators, in their turn, will be chosen on the basis of what they tell us about the influence of policy instruments on the final variables. What emerges here is a criterion for indicators that they be relatively closely related to the goal variables; relatively, here, means relative to the closeness of the targets. Let us refer to this criterion as $I1$ and state it formally as:

(I1) the indicator variables should have a direct, short, statistically firm, and theoretically unambiguous connection with the goal variables.

But all is not well with this single condition, since, as we have defined the problem so far, the indicator is not only to tell us what is happening to the goal variables, but also it must give us some idea of what the policy influence has been. As it stands, all we get from condition (I1) is a measure of all influences on the final variables; in fact, there are exogenous influences on the final variables and, more seriously, exogenous influences on both the targets and the indicators, all of which will totally confuse our policy. Thus, a second condition, no doubt hard to meet in practice, must be included; an example might be (*I*2):

(*I*2)   that the indicators separate efficiently the determinants of *target* variables into exogenous and policy-determined components.

In other words, we choose our indicator for its closeness to the final variables and its ability to divide the influences of exogenous factors from the policy factors, as determinants of the targets.

We would not need this second condition, then, if the targets could be uniquely hit by the monetary authorities; since this is generally not the case with the sort of targets generally proposed (such as 'free reserves', excess reserves, or, of course, the interest rate), we must fall back on condition (*I*2) or its equivalent. The advantage of this approach is that, in place of 'full-information' models, one is able to work with the monetary sector alone, at least if the interactions between fiscal and monetary policy are ignored. This information is better and more quickly obtained. On the other hand, a lot of exact information is still required and, of course, one must choose the correct targets and indicators or the economy may be destabilised rather than stabilised. For example, if we read a target, achieved at time t, as an indicator applying to time $t+1$, we may end up responding to our own policy actions. Indeed, we considered just this disadvantage above, when we talked about employing the interest rate as a target (in effect) when the authorities were shown to react to the effect of their inflationary push by giving a further push in the same direction. An indicator, such as the money stock, would have helped in such a case. Before turning to a broad assessment of the influence of monetary variables (and prices) on the economy we will consider, in the appendix to this chapter, what the literature on targets and indicators tells us about this vital choice.

APPENDIX TO CHAPTER 3: THE LITERATURE ON THE TARGETS–INDICATORS DISTINCTION: AN APPRAISAL

There are numerous studies on monetary indicators, but only a small number use a scheme in any way similar to the one discussed in this chapter. While this implies that the final evidence on the subject must be drawn from a very wide literature indeed, we will concentrate here on four studies which work on the issues, in the more systematic way the problem seems to require. In the next chapter we will consider much of that broader literature.

Most of the papers discussed here are monetarist in their conclusions and it seems appropriate to begin with a strong contribution from that area, that of Anna J. Schwartz [98]. Actually, Mrs Schwartz essentially eliminates the distinction between targets and indicators; in her view, an ideal *target* ought to be judged by three criteria:

(1)   is it measurable?
(2)   is it subject to control by central banks? and
(3)   is it a reliable indicator of monetary conditions?

Then, on the basis of her look at the data for U.K., Canadian, and Japanese central banks, she finds that the money stock is the best 'target–indicator', among a variety of potential candidates. Mrs Schwartz's criteria cannot be reconciled with the scheme described above, but they could be appropriate if the authorities could hit their targets without exogenous influences and if, of course, condition ($I1$) could be met. This case is thus a degenerate one, in effect, and, on the basis of even a casual inspection of the data, is untenable; the monetarist empirical tests also provide some contradiction to the methodology proposed by Mrs Schwartz although not, as it turns out, of her conclusions.

In another paper, de Leeuw and Kalchbrenner proposed that an indicator be chosen in terms of the following two conditions [66]:

($LK1$)   the Federal Reserve should exert a heavy and direct influence on it, and

(*LK*2) the variable should not respond contemporaneously to events in the private and 'other government' sectors. By the scheme in this chapter, (*LK*1) is a target condition and (*LK*2) is a target condition which, if met, will eliminate the need for the indicators to meet condition (*I*2). Such a variable is exogenous, in effect, and the chances of any known candidates meeting these conditions seems remote. Further, condition (*LK*2) raises the problem of an 'exogenous' influence which is especially hard to deal with; namely the interaction between the fiscal and monetary authorities [94, 99], which is evident at every step of the way in an active monetary policy.

The ranking test in this literature is that of Michael W. Keran [61] and it covers the six countries of the United States, Canada, West Germany, Japan, South Africa, and the United Kingdom, although the emphasis is on the United States. The general purpose of the indicator, Keran argues, after Brunner and Meltzer [14], is to 'scale' monetary and fiscal influences on economic activity, where 'scaling' is meant to imply measuring the impact of the instruments on the final variables. In particular, Keran argues that an indicator should

(*K*1) be responsive to the monetary tools of the central bank,

(*K*2) have a theoretically unambiguous association (or sign) with total demand, and

(*K*3) have a high degree of statistical association (with the theoretically correct sign) with the final variables.

Here we see conditions (*K*2) and (*K*3) representing condition (*I*1), and condition (*K*1) as essentially the target condition (*T*1), although it is stated in an imprecise way. There is thus a potential confusion of roles here, but Keran avoids it by employing only (*K*2) and (*K*3) in his actual tests; this, in turn, could not possibly throw a full light on the targets–indicators problem, although it could throw some on the gross effect of either instruments or intermediate variables on the final variables.

The actual equation tested by Keran is given here as equation (3.1), in first differences, that is

$$\Delta Y = a_0 + a_1 \Delta M + a_2 \Delta F + \gamma. \qquad (3.1)$$

The variables which determine Y (a variable) are either monetary (M) or fiscal (F), This expression will be (and is by Keran) recognised as the 'monetary multiplier' equation described as equation (4.1) in Chapter 4. The equation is tested using the monetary variables one at a time while observing the effect on the fit of the equation; thus, in effect, we ask the question, given fiscal influences, what intermediate monetary variable dominates the determination of changes in income? Lags are imposed by means of the Almon scheme [1, 59] in order to capture the delays in the effects which are, of course, an essential part of the policy problem.

Keran concludes, in spite of generally poor statistical fits that the money stock is the better indicator. But in equation (3.1) condition $(K1)$ is not applied in any way, and, in fact, we have a mixture of fiscal instruments (almost) and monetary indicators. It is surely important, if a variable is going to be used as both a target and an indicator, that it be easily hit, but even so, by stating condition $(K1)$, Keran is acknowledging that a variable may be very closely related to the goals, but impossible to hit, in which case it may be a relatively poor indicator by his rules. Clearly, as the interest rate can be very easily influenced (and quickly) compared to the money stock, Keran's conclusions could be even upset by his own rules.[1]

J. Ernest Tanner has gone over the same ground as Keran,

[1]In a paper by Hamburger [48] a similar type of test was undertaken on U.S. data; the equation tested by a second-degree polynomial is

$$\Delta \log_t \text{G.N.P.} = a + \sum_{i=1}^{n} b_i \Delta \log M_{t-i} + \gamma.$$

The results were especially good for total reserves (T.R.), the monetary base (B) [2, 61], narrow money (M_1), and bank credit (B.C.), with the latter dominating both M_1 and M_2.

for the U.S. data [105]. His conditions for the indicator variables are five in number.

($\mathcal{J}$1) the indicators should be highly responsive to the instruments ($K1, T1$);

($\mathcal{J}$2) the indicators should have a theoretically unambiguous sign with economic activity ($K2, I1$);

($\mathcal{J}$3) the indicators should be readily observable;

($\mathcal{J}$4) the association with final demand ought to be statistically close ($K3, I1$); and

($\mathcal{J}$5) the shorter the time lag between the indicator and economic activity, the better ($I1$).

We note that these conditions are a blend of the target–indicator conditions proposed above, except for the essential ($I2$) which can, of course, be dropped if exogenous forces do not affect the targets. In this respect, Tanner actually removes

			$\bar{R}^2$ For			
Period	N.B.R.	T.R.	B	M_1	M_2	B.C.
1953–68	0·32	0·44	0·34	0·39	0·28	0·39
1953–60	0·23	0·43	0·30	0·26	0·14	0·31
1961–8	0·22	0·31	0·21	0·31	0·43	0·45

N.B.R. is net borrowed reserves and M_2 is broad money. This, like the Keran test, is a test of the closeness of the indicator to the goal variables; it is also a test of 'monetary multipliers'. Whether the variables are exogenously determined or not is not tested in this paper. If they were, one could claim a 'target–indicator' in the tradition of the monetarist literature described above.

Another paper of the same vintage [114] looks at the reliability of M or i when they are embedded in, variously, four large-scale econometric models. When M is growing, but at different rates, and government expenditure always increase, i tends to give more incorrect information than M in the sense of predicting the sign of the change in income which results. When, however, M changes direction from quarter to quarter, i tends to perform better than M. These results, basically monetarist in their implications, come from complete models of the economy which are Keynesian in nature, as well as having explicit interest-rate transmissions for monetary policy. This last is also a Keynesian preoccupation.

exogenous and fiscal influences from his final demand data before considering the various indicators; this scheme, which is also effected by means of the Almon polynomial, is for exogenous forces identified as changes in exports only. Tanner's results are extensive and, at times, inconsistent with each other. He has made no use of the targets–indicators distinction and, also, has not met his first indicators condition; nevertheless, by removing the exogenous and fiscal influences on final demand, he has gone a long way toward treating the basic problem raised in this chapter. The fact that exogenous influences can affect the targets is, of course, not dealt with by Tanner.

Tanner offers the following general ranking of the popular indicators, with the best at the top of the list. These are, again, strongly monetarist results:

(1)   money stock or monetary base – rated 'acceptable–very good',

(2)   neutralised money stock [51] or monetary full employment interest rate [103] – rated 'acceptable–good', and

(3)   interest rate – rated 'unacceptable'.

As he notes himself, these are ranked by conditions ($\mathcal{J}3$) to ($\mathcal{J}5$) alone, rather than by the entire set. This might actually be a sound procedure, although no doubt not intended to be so, since the first condition, at least, is a target condition by the scheme proposed in this chapter. We turn to a more careful discussion of the links between money and economic activity in Chapter 4 before considering the targets problem more carefully in Chapter 5.

4 The Effects of Money and Prices on Economic Activity

INTRODUCTION

The model presented in Chapter 2 is a simple one, and it no doubt overstates the influence of the monetary authorities, but it is a widely employed one nevertheless. As noted earlier, both the Keynesians and their opponents, either monetarists or 'accelerationists', have adopted this framework and, as a consequence, much of the evidence concerning the effects of money (or of monetary policy) on the economy has been presented in papers taking one or the other of these polar positions. What follows in this chapter is, first, a discussion of what is probably the mainstream debate – that over 'monetary multipliers' – and, secondly, more general statements of the roles of money, monetary policy and inflation in the economy.

THE MONETARIST CONTROVERSY

The original rules of the game, essentially of an empirical nature, were laid down in a paper for the United States Commission on Money and Credit by Milton Friedman and David Meiselman [43]. Putting the matter somewhat baldly the question was asked which two relations, equation (4.1) describing the monetary multiplier (V') or equation (4.2), describing an autonomous multiplier (K') best explains economic activity (Y) over a variety of actual situations. The two equations are

$$Y = a + V'M, \tag{4.1}$$

and
$$Y = b + K'A. \tag{4.2}$$

In the Friedman and Meiselman paper, by their definitions of M (broad money) and A (net investment plus the government deficit plus the net foreign balance), and with consumption substituted for income,[1] a convincing victory went to equation (4.1) in terms of the tightness and stability of fit, with the former judged by the multiple correlation coefficient and the latter, somewhat casually, by the stability of the coefficient values over time, judged by an inspection of an arbitrary arrangement of sub-periods.

Both M and A are regarded as exogenous in the Friedman–Meiselman test and it is over the exogeneity of M, and of parts of A, that a lot of economists, monetarists and otherwise, have parted company with Friedman and Meiselman. We have already given some reasons for worrying about the exogeneity of the money stock in preceding chapters, and the subject will come up again at various points, but for now we should emphasise that it is on account of an active *and partly ineffective* monetary policy, conducted in partial ignorance of its effect and in terms of operating rules which are often inappropriate, which loosens the theoretical tie between policy and goal, whatever the actual correlation [25]. But the exact measurement of A and M are also debated in the literature, accepting the Friedman and Meiselman rules of the game, in a way which confounds any attempt to procure firm conclusions from the debate. For instance, the choice between narrow money and broad money (including time deposits) or even broader money (for example using Post Office savings [110]), is an issue which is hotly debated by economists under the heading of the 'definition of money'.[2] The Friedman–Meisel-

---

[1]This substitution can be justified with reference to the permanent-income hypothesis, $C = \alpha Y_p$, although, in fact, Friedman and Meiselman do this to avoid the double-counting inherent in the fact that $Y = C + A$ in their model. Ando and Modigliani express reservations about this [3].

[2]In several papers with a monetarist tone, equations exactly like equations (3.1) and (4.1) have been tested – with time lags even – in order to estimate by empirical means the 'moneyness' of time deposits. That is, assuming that narrow money is 'money', a

man approach to the definition of money is in favour of simple empirical tests, as a later study has explained [39]. On the definition of A, the issues are not so easily clarified, since what is exogenous here obviously depends on the scope of the model one has at one's disposal, or, worse, at the back of one's mind [21]. In the two well-known papers which responded to the original Friedman–Meiselman paper, while other issues were raised, the question of bias introduced by ignoring the endogenous components of M and A, particularly the latter, cause the authors to claim that the sharpness of the Friedman–Meiselman results were a special case and not at all general. Subsequent work has, provisionally, tended to confirm this view [11, 26, 49, 56].[1]

---

regression which includes as a second independent variable the quantity of time deposits will produce a coefficient for the latter which, when compared to the estimated coefficient for money gives the relative 'moneyness' of time deposits. The dependent variable is generally national income. The very same equation appears above as an indicator equation, in Chapter 3 (p. 40). The collapsing of three separate parts of the monetary problem into one basic relationship is typical of what might be termed 'strong monetarism'.

[1]Recent contributions, with some backsliding, have opened up some new lines of activity, creating the hope that the debate will, at long last, move on. While papers by Christ [21] and Poole and Kornbluth [88] are in the older tradition, they do succeed in raising some new points. Christ tests the reduced form of a self-consciously unspecified macroeconomic model over a long range of U.S. data (1891–1970) and concludes that, while both government purchases and high-powered money have had substantial effects on the economy, this effect has not been constant and, indeed, has weakened considerably in recent years. These results suggest, again, that fiscal or monetary policy, or even automatic stabilisers, may have been at work successfully in recent years. The Poole and Kornbluth paper uses the original equations of Friedman and Meiselman and those of their early critics, including Andersen and Jordan, to attempt predictions of the post-1963 G.N.P. data. The results are described as 'disappointing' in that a discretionary policy based on any of these simple relations would not earn much confidence; they were, though, evenly matched, if that is any consolation.

One would have thought that, since the related and basic questions of endogeneity and stability were raised as early as 1965, special activity would have occurred in that sector, but, in fact, studies along the Friedman–Meiselman lines have continued to pour out, justifying the descriptive term 'Monetarist' which has come into general usage to refer to much of this work. The best known of the monetarist papers is that of Andersen and Jordan [2] which uses, in addition to the money stock, a St Louis (Federal Reserve Bank) measure of the influence of money termed the 'monetary base' to provide empirical support to the following propositions: that the response of economic activity to monetary actions is (1) larger, (2) more predictable, and (3) faster than the response to fiscal actions.[1] But the same objections as discussed earlier can be raised against their procedure. Other studies have not been so sanguine, and when other countries are included in the sample, notably by Argy [4, 5], but also in another St Louis study [61], it is clear that any generalisation must carry extensive references to the local institutional conditions and, specifically, careful reference to the actual practices of the monetary authorities. It is possibly only in the case of fairly rapid inflation that money can satisfactorily be treated as an exogenous variable [18].

The results just described are from 'single-equation' models in which, like equation (4.1), the causation is assumed to run from money to economic activity; money is, further, taken to be an exogenous variable,[2] an assumption which 'completes'

[1]Much of the work on the 'indicators' of monetary policy, as discussed in Chapter 3, uses the same methodology as the Andersen–Jordan study, and for a variety of countries. Indeed, the Andersen–Jordan paper is itself referred to in the literature as an 'indicators' study, although the purpose of the test, as the conclusions exhibited here bear out, was to contribute to the Friedman–Meiselman debate.

[2]Actually, for much of U.S. history (at least) it is readily admitted by the monetarists [17, 37] that the money stock has other important determinants. Cagan notes that while gold dominates in the period up to 1914, there are periods (usually of crisis) even in the earlier

the model. Even if we could agree that there is a lead of money over activity [40], as it turns out, the anti-monetarist camp has an answer; this is best phrased by Tobin [106]. He sets out to explain how the lead of money over prices, an admittedly unstable and uncertain relation at best [40], can be explained without reference to aggressive and/or misguided monetary policy. He argues that the expectation of an increase in business activity, for example an expectation by business investors, could provoke a response first in the financial markets, as firms bid for the working capital they need, and then in the commodity and factor markets, as they bid for labour, materials, and capital goods. The former pressure will tend to be associated with an increase in the money stock, provided by the authorities passively and by the private economy in response to the tendency towards higher interest rates, and the latter will tend to drive up prices directly. Referring to the *ISLM* world of Chapter 2, the monetarist position suggests that money national income is dominated by shifts of the *LM* curve, while the contrasting view – allowing that the *LM* curve might shift as well – suggests that the dominant disturbances come from shifts in the *IS* curve [104.]

The problem which arises, using the real income model embodied in Figure 2 (p. 21), is essentially an identification problem, complicated by the inevitable lags between cause and effect. We may suppose we started at point $\tilde{c}$, in full equilibrium, and ended up at $\tilde{b}$, again in full equilibrium, but with higher prices, higher money interest rates, and a larger nominal money stock. Then, it is clear that we could have reached this point as the 'result' of a shift in the *LM* curve to the left (as a result of the rise in prices *or* as a result of an

---

period when fluctuations in the currency–deposit and reserve–deposit ratios dominate. These ratios are endogenously determined and, no doubt, highly influenced by business conditions. The Great Crash of the 1929–33 period saw another such episode, although it is certainly argued by the monetarists (see especially [37]) that the problems became serious mostly on account of the actions of the authorities.

increase in the demand for money) along with a rightward shift of the *IS* curve (whether an explicit change in aggregate demand occurred *or* as the result (see Figure 3 on p. 24) of the expectation that the rate of inflation would increase). The results, while they may be clearly interpreted in terms of shifts of functions in many cases, cannot be further decomposed into prime causes, since the shifts themselves have a variety of explanations. The results, that is to say, do not always give a clear indication of the causes.

MONEY AND INTEREST RATES

To this point, we have established that, even if we can convince ourselves that 'money leads prices', the lag is variable and the influence is of uneven magnitude [38, 40, 42]; indeed, Friedman argues this point as a critical defect of trying to control economic activity by means of monetary policy [38, 42, 44]. This result points us in the direction of studying the 'transmission mechanism' between changes in the money stock (whether policy determined or not) and changes in the final variables; this involves a detailed study of financial markets and of the effects of changes in interest rates and 'real balances' on spending and on asset choices.[1]

We will take up the formal modelling of the effect of money on interest rates in Chapter 5, where it will be seen to depend on (a) the speed of adjustment (or length of the lag) of the real versus the monetary sector, and (b) the relevant elasticities of demand and supply in both markets. Here, instead, we will refer to a wider range of studies whose purpose is to lay out the broad lines of this influence, while retaining as much of the richness of the financial structure as possible. The Keynesian view has always been a broad one here [5, 9, 35, 74, 82], and although monetarists readily admit the complexity of the problem [17, 37], they also warn us that there is a 'forest and

[1]This is a study of the 'intermediate lag' between changes in policy instruments and changes in financial variables, and of the 'outside lag' between the financial variables and the final activity.

trees' problem. Let us consider the case of a monetary restriction to clarify the issues.

If the authorities attempt to wring the neck of the monetary bird by open-market sales, it is clear that bond prices will tend to fall and yields to rise in the markets immediately affected. It is also clear that the monetary base will shrink. If the 'credit available' to the system is linked directly to the monetary base, then the credit available to borrowers will decline. Thus a combination of rising interest rates, reflecting both a rise in the cost of capital and a shortage of credit, will cause, in due course, a shortfall of spending on both investment and consumer goods. Furthermore, bond holders who were forced to sell out at the time of falling bond prices will have suffered capital losses in so far as other bonds react sympathetically to the original push by the government, and these 'wealth effects' could react on real spending in the same direction as the interest rate effect [84, 96].

Keynesians, in the early days, were likely to base their contradictions not on the causes just described, but on the magnitudes of the effects; indeed, just this description of events can be found in the works of Keynes [67]. It is argued, that is to say, that the 'price' effects of interest-rate changes on investment and consumption are negligible and, perhaps worse, are of uncertain size and length of lag. One certainly can agree that an *a priori* case for a particular magnitude is hard to establish and that, indeed, investment decisions, particularly those concerning fixed capital, will be sluggish in response to price changes alone. But working capital, which is constantly being refinanced, might easily respond quite quickly so that the general case is hard to establish. Further, under the circumstances, it would seem that a sudden cut in short-term interest rates would be less effective than a rise.[1]

[1]There is another part to the transmission problem here, involving the relation between short- and long-term interest rates. Monetary policy is generally conducted in short-term securities and if long-term rates are determined by investors who interpret a rise in short rates as a signal that long rates are to rise, they will sell their long-term bonds, thus confirming their expectation. In this

Returning to the special case of the 'tight-money' policy, we can now develop a second line of transmission, that which considers the role of financial intermediaries as (a) frustrators of monetary policy and (b) suppliers of a large part of the credit available to the economy. As interest rates rise, and the rationing of credit begins to occur in financial markets, individuals will, in response to higher yields, switch their assets from idle cash to intermediary deposits. The cash will, of course, find its way back into the banking system, but more lending will be enabled; economic activity, in so far as it is linked to the total quantity of credit rather than to its price, will thereby not be affected appreciably by the tight-money policy. In the words of the Radcliffe Committee, the velocity of money is 'potentially infinite' under these circumstances [89]. There is another aspect to this process and that is one of deliberate 'intermediation'; as interest rates rise, new institutions will spring up and old ones will diversify and extend their activities [57, 89]. Indeed, the supply of credit to the financial markets, at least, is potentially 'institution elastic' so that, at least, tight money could be hard to impose on the economy.

Whether or not this over-all frustration to monetary policy occurs, there is evidence to suggest that particular sectors are affected by the scramble for credit which follows hard on the heels of a credit squeeze. Perhaps the most widely held view here is that tight money tends to channel funds away from the housing sector; certainly the 1966 and 1969–70 'credit crunches' in the United States are alleged to have had this characteristic, and social legislation, to try to protect the sources of funds of

---

case, long-term rates will move with short-term rates and the price effect in the short-term market will be directly transmitted to the long-term capital market, possibly quite quickly. Indeed, the 'bills-only' policy of the U.S. monetary authorities was justified in these terms [91, 113], when it was in vogue. If speculators operate differently, or if long rates are especially sluggish, the forces will not spread quickly and, incidentally, the opportunity to adopt a different policy in the capital market (long) to that followed in the money market will arise. This policy was known as 'operation twist' in its time [93].

the intermediaries involved in lending to the private housing sector, has been enacted [12]. A variation of this argument has tight money adversely affecting small businesses, a claim often disputed by bankers themselves.

It also appears that sometimes the stock market is sharply affected by monetary policy, whether anticipated or actual. The principal reason appears to be the fact that changes in the quantity of money imply changes in credit available for the purchase of common stocks, in the same direction. Part of this is a deliberate part of policy, no doubt, and to reinforce this effect, instruments like the U.S. 'margin requirements' exist, and are frequently employed [80]. More generally, to the extent that monetary policy is uneven, unpredictable, destabilising, irrational, or just plain disturbing (perhaps because of vigorous 'announcement effects'), costs are imposed on every part of the private sector, and even on the government in its budgetary operations, in the form of increased uncertainly. Furthermore, over-reaction can occur and expectations can be altered; if the expectations are translated into some kind of covering action, further, often undesirable, effects, may well occur.[1] The stock market, thus, is only one among a number of markets affected because its view of what is to come is altered as monetary policy changes direction.

THE EFFECTS OF INFLATION [36, 50, 71]

To this point we have concentrated on the 'real' side of things, at least in the sense of thinking about the effects of changes in the stock of money (given prices), but it is just as well to

[1]To the extent that monetary policy affects consumer spending evenly, it might be said to operate in an ideal way but, if consumers react to unexpected changes in their wealth (or prospects) by first withholding or increasing expenditures on consumer durables, certain vital sectors – vital because the potential for accelerator–multiplier effects seems greater – may be adversely affected [74]. In recent years the automobile industry seems to have taken up some of the slack here, notably in the recession which began in 1974. Of course, energy problems were also part of that situation.

note, particularly in these inflationary days, that there are quite specific costs and benefits associated with a rapid change in prices by themselves, whether induced by monetary changes, by expectations, or by both. The following collection is derived from an excellent survey of the literature by Edward Foster [36].

The major problems arise because of distortions between items whose money prices are fixed versus items whose money prices can vary. Thus, if the rate of inflation is imperfectly anticipated, there will be (a) more frequent and, presumably, costly adjustments in fixed-term agreements designated in money terms (labour contracts leap to mind) or (b) an unexpected redistribution of resources, and (c) a situation in which money interest rates will not perfectly reflect the anticipated inflation, with consequent distortions in capital markets. Indeed, these factors increase with increasing fluctuations in the rate of inflation. But even if the rate of inflation is perfectly anticipated, there will be a reallocation of resources from the future to the present, which will affect the rate of growth adversely (it may, of course, stimulate an economy and set its accelerator–multiplier forces to work if the economy was stagnant to begin with).

The erosion of the value of money also forces an economising on items denominated in money terms and an 'uneconomic' specialisation in less-liquid assets, such as real property, as stores of value. The other side of this coin is that a government can finance part or all of its deficit by resort to 'inflationary finance' and, perhaps not incidentally, destroy undesirable vested interests in this way. These comments apply equally to sophisticated economies, where the central bank purchases some of the issue of the government, and to less-developed countries, where the 'finance motive' just described may dominate. Common stocks, widely thought to be a good hedge against inflation, come in for some attention here. Since corporations can be expected to profit from inflation, particularly if prices lead costs as they might in a demand-pull inflation, the dividend payout (and presumably the value of the common stock) could also be expected to keep pace with inflation. The other side of the coin is that whatever is expected to affect the economy in general ought to be expected to affect the average market value of all large firms in the economy. Thus, if it is felt that a rapid and variable inflation is undermining the economy, common stock prices could deteriorate – this may explain the bear market on major U.K., Canadian, and U.S. exchanges in 1974 (and on some accounts from 1965 or 1966).

As inflation gradually erodes real wages, workers, perhaps because of money illusion and perhaps because a job search involving unemployment is perceived to be a risky business in an uncertain time, increase (relatively) their supply of services to the market. This is stimulative and can be counted as a benefit. The other side of the coin is, probably, the painful adjustment of money to real wages, involving strikes and the like, which has become an increasing function of the rate of change of prices. We will return to these issues in the appendix to this chapter. Workers may suffer (and they may not), but the poorer groups actually seem to benefit from inflation, mainly because the employment effect just described dominates the effects on their meagre pensions and also because of the erosion of the value of their debts, such as they are.

Finally, there is the possibility, which none of us is allowed to take seriously, that an inflation will build into a hyperinflation with a resulting collapse of the economic system, itself imposing huge costs on nearly everyone.

CONCLUSION

This chapter has considered a large variety of the effects of excessive money production. While it has not been argued that excessive money production is the sole responsibility of the government, it has been emphasised that this is an important part of the monetarist view of the problem; indeed, some effort has been made here to show both sides of the argument. We may conclude, somewhat weakly that, whatever its causes, inflation is shown to be a serious problem. We turn to a more exact specification of the problems of conducting a monetary policy in Chapter 5, after a more detailed discussion of one of the effects of inflation (and possibly monetary policy) which has not received much attention in the literature.

APPENDIX TO CHAPTER 4: INFLATION AND THE DISTRIBUTION OF INCOME

In the foregoing, we have abstracted from one aspect of the monetary-inflation debate, and that is the more recent literature which comes under the heading of the 'accelerationist' hypothesis and its logical antithesis. A summary of the view, as proposed by Friedman [44] and attacked by Tobin [107] is carried in Bronfenbrenner [13]; the presentation here will consider, along with the arguments of Tobin, a synthesis suggested by the earlier work of Ball [9].

In recent years a number of countries have experienced fluctuations in the distribution of their income, mostly in favour of wage earners, and these changes appear to have been a direct result of either the accelerating rate of inflation or its causes. Figure 4 contains a picture of the wage share in national income for the United Kingdom, the United States and Canada: in all three cases there is an upward drift, and in all three cases there seems to be a distinct peak in the series. The U.S. peak is in the second quarter of 1972, and is at 75·7 per cent; the Canadian peak is in the second quarter of 1970, and is at 74·5 per cent; and the U.K. peak is in the third quarter of 1970, and is at 72·6 per cent. Put that way, the similarity is pronounced, and points one in the direction of common causes.

In the tradition of the monetarist literature, we may argue that, approximately, the deviation of the share from its long run value – whatever that might be – is the *result* of changes in the inflation rate (and its causes). The appropriate (approximate) test, then, is to regress the share on a constant, representing the long-run share, and the inflation rate. The latter should be suitably lagged to represent the lag-in-effect which

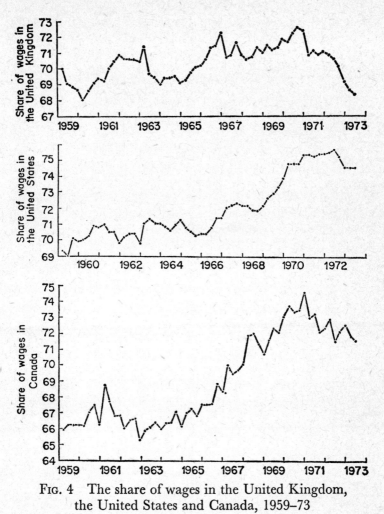

FIG. 4   The share of wages in the United Kingdom,
the United States and Canada, 1959–73

is to be expected in this sort of situation. Equation (4.3) is the estimating equation proposed, where T represents the (arbitrary) length of the lag tried, that is

$$S_{wt} = \alpha + \sum_{i=t-1}^{t-T} B_i \left(\frac{\Delta P}{P} \right)_{t-i} + \gamma. \qquad (4.3)$$

55

Table 1 contains a summary of the results for the three countries described in Figure 4, using the Almon lag scheme [1, 59]. It is clear that the association is generally a strong one, although there are some anomalies.

As Figure 4 indicates, the experiences of the countries differ, with the U.S. and Canadian results showing sharp peaks, while the behaviour of the U.K. share is much less decisive, actually ending up at a lower point than it started. If one hypothesises, as equation (4.3) does, that the cause of the situation is variations in the rate of inflation, then the U.K. result in Table 1 is also unlike the U.S. and Canadian ones. The lack of similarity shows up in the sign of the summed lag coefficients – which is negative in the U.K. case – and in the quality of the fit of the equation – which is good in the U.S. and Canadian cases, and poor in the U.K. case.

The most popular explanation of these events seems to be

TABLE 1

The effect of the inflation rate
on the wage share of three industrial countries

	United States	Canada	United Kingdom
Constant	69·22	63·54	76·95
(*t*-value)	(625·9)	(167·8)	(28·60)
Sum of coefficients	5·39	10·01	− 6·30
(*t*-value)	(29·1)	(25·0)	(1·80)
Mean lag in periods	10·74	10·64	——
$\bar{R}^2$	0·988	0·949	0·827
Degree of equation	6	6	5
Total lag in quarters	21	21	32
Durbin–Watson statistics	1·64	2·22	1·50

Source: the data employed are the same as used in Figure 4 (p. 55), from 1959 through to the second quarter of 1973. The wage share is the percentage of national income going to wage earners; the price index used is the Consumer Price Index. The test statistic used to obtain the best-fitting degree and length of lag for the Almon polynomial was the coefficient of determination ($\bar{R}^2$).

the 'strong-unions' hypothesis. Quite simply, it is argued that increasingly strong unions, in the process of forcing up their shares, also force up the rate of inflation; thus, at face value, unions are at work in the United States and Canada, but not in the United Kingdom. Aside from not fitting the facts (about unions) in all likelihood, there are three theoretical problems with this view. The first, quite simply, is that the fact that an identifiable economic group profits from a situation is in no way proof that it brought about the situation. In particular, a third agency, for example the government, may have brought about the situation for reasons of its own. The second problem is that the view just described has an implicit timing relationship – notably that changes in relative shares, as the proximate cause of the accelerated inflation, might reasonably be expected to precede changes in the rate of inflation, rather than to follow them. This was quite possibly not true in the U.S. and Canadian cases, although no proof is offered here; that is, equation (4.3) *assumes* that inflation leads the change in the share. The third problem is that normally one would expect aggressive union activity to produce higher wages (and possible higher prices) and more unemployment. Since the share of labour is calculated as the wage times the quantity employed (divided by total national income) and the former is rising while the latter is falling, the ambiguous relationship between the share of labour and the inflation rate implied by this theory is not much use in explaining the precise and firm positive relationship showing for the United States and Canada. Of course, the U.K. result seems more plausible in this case. Let us consider two models of special use in dealing with the other two countries.

The first model is a 'validated cost-push' model. The general idea behind this view is that increases in real wages, which normally generate forces to reverse their thrust, are validated by the monetary-fiscal authorities because the unemployment which is observed to result is deemed undesirable [19]. We may suppose that because of union pressure there is some leftward shift of the supply curve of labour. Assuming that both factor supply curves (labour and capital) are perfectly

57

inelastic (for clarity rather than because it is necessary to the argument), this leftward shift creates unemployment of both capital and labour: to the capital sector it will appear as a fall in the demand for capital (assuming capital and property are gathered together as the residual share). The authorities react by increasing their rate of production of money and this increases aggregate demand; we may argue that both of the factor demand curves shift to the right. If the exact amount of the new unemployment is eliminated by the policy and if there has been no substitution of capital for labour and no significant technical change in the meantime, the same quantity of capital will be employed as before, at the same rate; total payments to capital will be unchanged. On the other hand, the new labour supply schedule, higher than the old, will have been validated by the increase in aggregate demand; the result is an increase in total payments to labour, a rise in the share of labour, and, of course, a step-up in the rate of inflation. The sequence one might observe is (1) a rise in prices and in unemployment, (2) an increase in the rate of growth of the money stock as monetary policy moves to validate the price increase, and (3) a rise in the share of labour to the extent that the monetary policy works in the sense of increasing aggregate demand. Prices could rise still further at this stage, especially if expectations become aroused. Thus the reason that the rate of inflation is related to the distribution of income is not a direct one and, indeed, would not occur if the relation were not validated by the monetary policy. The results in Figure 4 and Table 1, thus, could indicate that in the United States and Canada a strong validation occurred, while in the case of the United Kingdom, either union activity dominated, or unemployment was let slip, at least in so far as monetary policy is concerned.

A contrasting view of the causal sequence is now known as the 'accelerationist hypothesis' [44]. If one supposes that there is a 'natural' rate of unemployment (not necessarily a constant) then any efforts to establish a rate in contradiction to this natural rate will set up powerful contradictory forces. Suppose, for example, that the natural rate of visible male unemployment were to rise, perhaps because women were entering the labour force in greater numbers or because of some technological change. Whatever the cause, the result will be perceived by the authorities, who will increase the money stock, causing prices to rise. In the first instance, the share going to labour need not rise, but it certainly will if there is some further factor causing the quantity of workers employed to increase (or not decrease in proportion). No doubt the strongest card in Friedman's suit would be an expansion in the demand for labour caused by the fall in real wages; this, presumably, comes about because prices are rising faster than money wages. Friedman then tacks on another important detail: workers will not perceive that real wages are falling (because they will be satisfied with their perceived rise in money wages) and will increase their supply of services to the market.[1] On both accounts, labour's share is increased by (what appears to be the cause) inflation. Labour 'wakes up' to the situation, of course, and in the course of raising its supply price causes

[1]Tobin's counter-attack on this position is not so much a direct one, as it was on the earlier monetarist ideas, but more of a set of qualifications, leading one into a different direction [107]. First, he notes that in a non-centralised economy in which 'sticky' money wages cannot fall, inflation is the only way real wages can be reduced. Secondly, short-run involuntary unemployment or over-employment can arise in an economy as the labour force adjusts to a new long-run situation without any need to refer to the mechanism of 'money illusion' in the supply function of labour services as Friedman does. In particular, while workers may accept jobs above the 'natural' rate of employment as a result of overvaluing their real wage, it is also likely that they are overvaluing their planned expenditures as well. Thus it is not obvious that they will increase their services as the accelerationist view requires, at least for a clear case. Turning to the question of 'stagflation', Tobin argues (a) that the principal agent is the effect of disequilibria in product markets on labour markets in increasing unemployment and (b) that the effect of 'floors' (still not money illusion) on wages is (on net) inflationary by a kind of ratcheting effect, irrespective of the state of aggregate demand. This last comes out very much like a version of the 'creeping-inflation' hypothesis of the 1950s.

unemployment to crop up again; this time the pace of money-induced inflation has to step up (since labour will now expect the old rate of inflation to persist) to mop up a specific quantity of unemployment; this explains the tag 'accelerationist' and provides an alternative explanation of the results in Table 1 and Figure 4, at least for the United States and Canada.

5 Uncertainty and the Lag-in-Effect of Monetary Policy

INTRODUCTION

While the question of various types of instability concerns all aspects of the monetary-policy problem, there is one special case which has, since the monetarists first raised the issue, dominated the discussion. This is the question of which *target* (an interest rate or a measure of the money stock) should the authorities aim their operating instruments at. In Chapter 6 we will consider what the actual choices have been in the United Kingdom and the United States, but here, because it is basic to an intelligent formulation of policy, we will seek to discover what the general issues are. Underlying all this will be the fact that any policy must be formulated in partial ignorance of the actual workings of the economy, a state which must exist because the causes of events are uncertain, and because events follow causes only after long (and variable) lags.

In an early, but now largely extinct, literature, the problem of a choice of target which we face here was tied up with the notion of a 'natural' rate of interest. If there is a natural rate, at which saving and investment are equated without inflation, then any attempt to assert a money rate of interest below this rate would involve the monetary authorities in the task of increasing the money supply, without limit so long as the condition persisted. The authorities could not, in this instance, pick a 'natural-rate' target, since the natural rate is only measurable after the fact (if at all) but they could pick a money-rate target easily enough. But then their problems begin. First, if they simply tried to hold the money rate of

61

interest constant in the face of a fluctuating natural rate, they would be contributing, variously, to an unstable money market; in this fashion 'real' disturbances would be transmitted to the monetary sector. Worse, because of the lags in the system, the real disturbances – say a shift of the investment function – could have been caused by an original monetary change in the first place. In other words, once the system is triggered, further cycles can be generated simply by the authorities' responses to the results of their past actions [37].

The second case, a variation on the theme, involves the sort of expectations we discussed in Chapter 2. Again, let us suppose that the observable money rate of interest includes a mark-up for the expected rate of change of prices, as in equation (2.12) (see p. 23). If the authorities observe, with disfavour, a rise in the money rate of interest, they may easily interpret it as a sign of tight money whatever its real cause; indeed, this may well be the case. Under the assumption of the 'stabilising' objective used in Chapter 2, they would react to this situation by increasing the rate of production of the money stock; an increase in the rate of growth of the money stock, *ceteris paribus*, will increase the rate of change of prices. This, in turn will tend to cause expectations of inflation to increase and the money rate of interest will tend to go up instead of down as the authorities had wished. Naturally, if they interpret the further rise in the interest rate as a further 'tightening' of the money market, they will continue this basically destabilising policy. These results, of course, are not invariant with respect to the cause of the initial rate rise, for a rise in interest rates could be correctly read as tighter money. But consider the case of a rise in the expected rate of inflation which is 'exogenously' triggered (perhaps because of an historically high union wage settlement or because of an oil crisis). In this case, the authorities' action has been to validate the expectation by producing the inflation which was anticipated. Further, in the absence of this validation, the pressure for higher prices, at least as regards the capital markets described here, would tend to abate.

A more general case can be made as well. If exogenous and

unpredictable influences affect the link between the policy instruments and the goal variables, then, depending on which market is hardest to predict, an interest-rate or a money-stock (or, ideally, a combination) target may be the best approach to adopt. Consider the simple *ISLM* model in Figure 5 [87]. In a completely deterministic world it makes absolutely no difference whether one aims at an interest-rate or a money-stock target. But suppose the *IS* function is subject to such (unknown) disturbances that its position can be anywhere between IS_1 and IS_2 in Figure 5. Suppose the operating goal of the authorities is Y_f, for full employment. Then, a policy

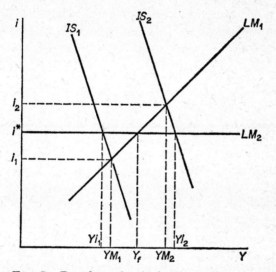

Fig. 5   Random shocks in the *IS* function

of maintaining the money stock at a particular level (M_1) will, *ceteris paribus*, produce an upward-sloping *LM* curve like LM_1 (the curve is drawn arbitrarily near the middle of the range of possible *IS* curves). Once we pick an *LM* curve, the stochastic behaviour of the *IS* curve, for the reasons given, takes over. We can obtain an actual *IS* curve anywhere between the two drawn; thus the actual level of income may lie anywhere between YM_1 and YM_2. The interest rate, of course, is destabilised, and lies anywhere between i_2 and i_1. Suppose, on the other hand, that we picked an interest-rate target of i^* to achieve the same level of income so that LM_2 resulted. In this case the potential variation in income is between Yi_1 and Yi_2, for the same potential variation in the IS curve. Clearly the money-stock target is superior in the case when the disturbance is along the IS curve.

But if the LM curve rather than the IS curve is subject to exogenous shocks or if the effect of exogenous shocks is larger on the LM curve than on the IS curve, the reverse conclusions could hold. Consider Figure 6; here we can argue that the demand for money function is unpredictable, leading to an LM_1 or an LM_2, or anything in between, if we pick a particular money-stock target. The result is a potential variation in income between YM_1 and YM_2. Because we are assuming that our selected targets can be hit, the selection of an interest-rate target, when it is fluctuations in the interest rate which are, essentially, the problem, will tend to stabilise the system at Y_f, since LM_3 will be the result of the stabilisation. The authorities will provide whatever money stock (which will, therefore, be destabilised) the market wants in order to achieve this result. Thus the interest-rate target is superior. There is an assymetry here, to be sure, because the shock in the first case is in the final market, and cannot be eliminated, while in the case of Figure 6, because it was in the intermediate financial sector, it was assumed to be eliminated completely, there being no link between the destabilised money stock and the IS curve.[1] Further, we are assuming that the targets can be hit without error, a serious violation of real-world conditions as they were described in Chapter 3.

---

[1] The argument for the destabilising behaviour caused by mis-reading a money interest rate as a real interest rate is not dealt with by this model, which asumes a constant price level. This, in effect, breaks the links between the money market and economic activity. Real balance effects [83] are, likewise, ruled out. These complications ought to be studied in this context.

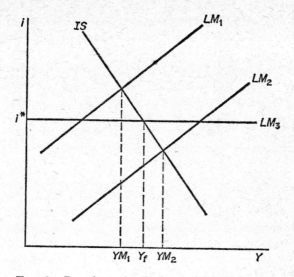

FIG. 6   Random shocks in the *LM* Function

THE EFFECT OF LAGS

The basic problem here, again raised by the early monetarists several decades ago, concerns the potential instability of a system in which lags – motivated in various ways – will appear. Now clearly, one can construct a system to do pretty nearly whatever one wants, so that it is not the issue. Rather the question concerns the relative stability of the models we actually use when these dynamic considerations are included. In the very simplest case, we ordinarily assume that the authorities determine their target variables (s), but so long as there is any lag in the adjustment of the final variables to a policy-induced change in either M or i, taken as a target, over-adjustment will occur in financial markets. For example, a change in the money stock will cause an over-reaction in interest rates because the pressure, not yet reaching the final variables, must be taken up somewhere [55, 64, 108]; that is what the previous section demonstrated.

The lags which we are considering are endemic in the macroeconomic-policy world, and no model would be complete without them [35]. In the first instance, the authorities will receive information about the objective variables some time after the event (an information lag), will pass it through their decision-making apparatus (a decision lag), and will act on it (an action lag); these elements make up what is now called the 'inside' lag of monetary policy. Once a policy change in the instruments has occurred, the intermediate financial variables will begin to be affected but with a lag which is called the 'intermediate' lag. Finally, the changes in financial markets will take some time to reach the final (objective) variables; this is often referred to as the 'outside' lag.

A number of problems immediately occur. In the first place, it is clear that the longer one waits for information, the better the information is likely to be. The other side of the coin is that the longer one waits, the longer the total lag between impulse and final correction. This last, in the second place, is a problem because the longer the total lag, the more likely it will be that the entire policy will be wrong. Wrongness, here, means too much, too little, or a movement in the wrong direction. In the third place, different instruments will have different lags, starting with the decision apparatus right through to the final variables. Consider the following scheme, which compares monetary policy (a) to fiscal policy (b):

(a) central bank→open-market operations→interest rates→ consumption plus investment decisions→employment;
(b) Treasury→Legislature→changes in tax rates→consumption plus investment decisions→employment.

Thus, we could argue, monetary policy (a) is faster in its early stages (up to the interest rate) and slower in its later stages, while fiscal policy (b) would normally be slower in its implementation but faster in its effect once it got going.

To see how outside lags might affect the system consider the following *ISLM* model in which a single lag has been imposed on the spending function ($E_t = C_t + I_t$) while none

66

has been imposed on the demand for money function. The model consists of

$$E_t = (1 - a) \ (a_1 + a_2 Y_t + a_3 i_t) + a E_{t-1}, \quad (5.1)$$

and
$$M_t = b_1 + b_2 Y_t + b_3 i_t. \quad (5.2)$$

In this model we are assuming that the monetary sector responds more quickly to pressure; we could have a lag on both equations, but the arithmetic is simpler without one on the demand for money. With a clearing equation for equation (5.1) of $Y_t = E_t$ and for equation (5.2) of $M_t = \bar{M}_t$ – which, in effect, is saying that the money stock is determined by the authorities – we can solve for the time path of income. The result is equation (5.3), that is

$$Y_t = \frac{a}{K_1} Y_{t-1} + \frac{K_2}{K_1}, \quad (5.3)$$

where
$$K_1 = 1 - (1 - a) a_2 + (1 - a) b_2 \frac{a_3}{b_3}, \text{ and}$$

$$K_2 = (1 - a) a_3 \frac{\bar{M}}{b_3} - (1 - a) b_1 \frac{a_3}{b_3} + (1 - a) a_1.$$

Shocks can be administered to this system in the form of changes in the parameters, particularly in a_1, b_1, and $\bar{M}$. The latter, of course, represents monetary policy. Equation (5.3) is a first-order difference equation in income, and the time path that income will follow depends on the value of a/K_1. We cannot say, *a priori*, what this will be, but several interesting cases emerge. Assume, for convenience, that $a_2 = b_2 = 1$; then the parameter in question becomes

$$\frac{a}{a + (1 - a) a_3 / b_3},$$

that is, the results depend on the length of the lag (a) and the two interest-rate effects jointly. Normally, with $a < 1$, this would produce a stable result ($a/K_1 < 1$) but if either a_3 or b_3 is positive (but not both) we will get an unstable result. Further,

67

if $a_3 = 0$, the value of a/K_1 is on the borderline of a value o unity. If $b_3 = 0$, that is if the demand for money does not depend on the interest rate, then the denominator approaches infinity and the result is stability. While the more general cases are more interesting, this model reveals the kind of results one can get here [75].

We may visualise the situation, and gain some additional insight into the problem, if we graph the above in the form of the *ISLM* diagram with short-run and long-run curves drawn in. In Figure 7, we depict a case in which there is an upward shift in the *IS* curve (it could come about as a result of fiscal policy or, of course, as the result of a change in a_1 in

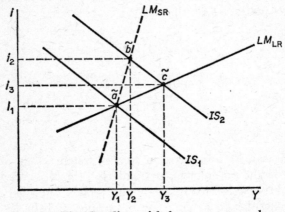

FIG. 7   Fiscal policy with long monetary lags

equation (5.1); here adjustment is seen as going (first) up the short-run *LM* curve (LM_{SR}), because here the lags are assumed to be longer in the money market, before that curve gradually pivots around (in the long run) to its final position as LM_{LR}). The movement in this case is $\tilde{a}$ to $\tilde{b}$ to $\tilde{c}$. Income, in this case, goes steadily from Y_1 to Y_2 to Y_3 – all increases – but the interest rate shoots up to i_2, an over-reaction, before falling back to i_3. Thus, while the interest rate does respond in the expected direction (upwards), its movement consists of two separate moves, one upwards and one downwards, and intermediate readings on its changes (as indicators) would indicate a sharper reaction than actually obtained in the first part, and a completely wrong reaction in the second. Of course, it is the over-reaction, because of the lag in adjustment in the monetary sector, which produced this cycle.

A monetary policy to raise income could exhibit the same tendency, as Figure 8 indicates; in this case, the spending sector has the slow reaction. Here we show the movement along a short-run IS curve (IS_{SR}) and, again, a cycle in the interest rate compared to that in income (which is again monotonically increasing), with the points of movement from $\tilde{a}$ to $\tilde{b}$ to $\tilde{c}$ again. Of course, these are special cases with, quite possibly, Figure 8

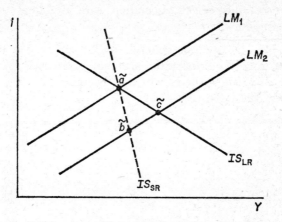

FIG. 8   Monetary policy with long spending lags

with its relatively slow adjustment of spending to a change in the money stock (an increase) being judged the more likely case.

In either case, however, the interest rate does not send off unambiguous signals, by itself. In Figure 8, as in Figure 7, there is a cycle in interest rates, so the 'indication' it would give would depend on when one observed it. As an indicator of what is happening to income in such cases the interest rate would be a poor bet, even if the cause of the original shift were known with certainty. In both cases the behaviour of the money stock, quite possibly in step with the growth of income (through equation (5.2)), would probably have been a better indicator.

We may conclude this chapter by emphasising the principal findings:

(a) the introduction of stochastic elements will affect our choice of instruments, depending on which sector is more affected by the disturbances;

(b) the introduction of lags raises the possibility of instability, depending on (i) the length of the lags and (ii) the parameters of the system; and

(c) the introduction of lags illustrates the main reason for the monetarist dislike of the interest rate as an indicator variable (its theoretical association with the final variables being ambiguous).

These results are not general, to be sure, since the 'lag problem' and the 'stochastic problem' were not combined; there is a literature here, which is beyond the scope of this study [55, 75, 81, 87, 108].

6 The International Setting of Monetary Policy: U.K. and U.S. Perspectives

INTRODUCTION

In this chapter our main topic will be a discussion of recent U.K. and U.S. monetary policy but, because the environment in which this policy has been conducted has often been dominated by international considerations, an extended discussion of the problems which this broader perspective requires will precede the policy survey [76, 111]. As we will see, the problems which countries face depend on the payments system adopted – and on how well it works – and any generalisation which leads to policy prescriptions has to be reworked in terms of what is likely to happen to the payments system. As these words are being written, we stand amid the wreckage of the International Monetary Fund (I.M.F.), observing a 'world-wide' inflation and a 'system' of managed flexibility. But things were not always this way, and as the basis of the discussion, we will investigate the I.M.F. in its successful period after the Second World War.

FROM BRETTON WOODS TO CHAOS

The I.M.F. grew out of a series of intense negotiations between the major Allied powers, negotiations which were conducted under a series of working assumptions which have since been falsified, at least in part. At the time (in 1944) it was generally

71

thought that the future would bring back the Great Depression – or at least a prolonged stagnation – as well as an immediate post-war inflation; stagflation, that is to say, is not a new worry. It was felt that whatever discipline could be imposed by the payments system ought to be encouraged, and a set of rules was drawn up which (a) frowned on persistent balance-of-payments deficits, (b) discouraged devaluations, and (c) provided for only a small increase in total reserves over time. The inflation came to pass, and the Korean War exacerbated it, but the stagnation did not; furthermore, international trade and capital flows grew in magnitude so rapidly that the system designed to deal with fluctuations in the hundreds of millions found itself in the billions and, in the 1970s, in the tens of billions. Since the means of payment were never to grow at a rate anything like this, it is small wonder that the system collapsed.

At the same time the I.M.F. was constructed, a large number of countries embarked on the new course of attempting to control domestic activity, particularly the expected increase in unemployment, by the recently minted tools of fiscal and monetary policy. Generally speaking, both internal and external goals were thought to be relevant and it was felt that with several instruments, several goals could be achieved at once. The role of the I.M.F. in all this was to provide a cushion, necessary under the system of fixed exchange rates with narrow bands drawn around the rates, in order to free instruments for use in domestic management. But the reserves in the system grew *relatively* scarce – and also tended to accumulate in the hands of surplus countries – so that the promise of the I.M.F. was never realised. Indeed, some countries, notably the United Kingdom and many less-developed countries, never seemed to get out of trouble.

As it turns out, even if a nation's 'exchange-equalisation' account is able to keep (along with its I.M.F. quota) the exchange rate within the bounds required, there are monetary repercussions. Namely, a balance-of-payments surplus will tend to increase the monetary base and a balance-of-payments deficit to decrease it, and, *ceteris paribus*, a domestic instrument will have to be employed to offset any undesirable repercussions here. Furthermore, if a balance-of-payments deficit is threatening to exhaust a nation's reserves, either a dampening of the economy by means of fiscal (and monetary) policy, or a sharp increase in interest rates to draw in capital from abroad, will tend to help. In this case, we see a foreign-exchange-created decline in the monetary base along with (say) open-market sales or rises in interest rates, all of which would cut charply into domestic demand – and employment. It is small wonder that the pressure from the deficit countries led to the reform – and quite possibly the collapse of the I.M.F. system – in the late 1960s.

There are some technical aspects to the use of monetary and fiscal policy which depend on whether one is living in a fixed or fluctuating exchange-rate system. In either case, we will assume that there are two goals [77] which are (a) *internal equilibrium* (price-level stability or unemployment), and, (b) *external equilibrium* which is made up of (i) balance-of-payments stability (fixed exchange-rate system), and, (ii) minimum exchange-rate fluctuations (flexible exchange-rate system). Further, we will assume that there are two instruments of policy which are, (a) *fiscal policy* (government surplus or tax rate), and, (b) *monetary policy* (interest rate change or open-market operations). Thus, the actual conclusions depend on which system is chosen, the values of the parameters of the system, and the relative mobility of capital between nations.

Under a fixed exchange-rate system like the one under discussion, there are four possible states of the world with respect to the two objectives: (i) balance-of-payments surplus with domestic inflation; (ii) balance-of-payments surplus with domestic deflation; (iii) balance-of-payments deficit with domestic inflation; and (iv) balance-of-payments deficit with domestic deflation. There can also, of course, be stability in either or both markets. In cases i and iii, the successful use of a contractionary fiscal policy to control inflation would shrink domestic incomes and lower prices (and lower the monetary base) as well as lead to lower interest rates. In case iii, all of this would be fine for the balance-of-payments

73

deficit but, in case I, the fiscal measure would tend to exacerbate the balance-of-payments surplus, at least with regard to the lower prices increasing exports. Similarly, if a country has a deflation, a stimulatory fiscal policy would tend to assist the elimination of a pesky surplus (case II), but worsen a deficit (case IV). Thus in two cases, I and IV, there must be another instrument if both goals are to be achieved, and in the other two cases this might still be the case.

The monetary instrument most widely used is thought to be the open-market operation, although the discussion of this issue tends to concentrate on the interest rate. If we do likewise, and acknowledge that a 'quantities' policy has a 'price' dimension, then it is relatively clear that the choice of whether to use the monetary instrument on the internal or the external objective in cases I and IV depends on the relative effectiveness of fiscal and monetary policy in the two situations. It is essentially an empirical question – on which much research has been done [62, 81, 101] – but, under simplified conditions, a clear case can be made for using the monetary weapon (changes in interest rates) on the external problem and the fiscal weapon on the internal problem, ignoring the interaction between the two [77]. The key to this result is that one can argue that the interest rate is relatively good in drawing off foreign capital to help out a payments crisis and that fiscal policy – once under way – can be relatively quick-acting on final spending. Certainly the United Kingdom and Canada, while their fiscal policies have often been rudimentary, have often employed the monetary weapon in this way.

This is not the place to conduct a discussion of the advantages and disadvantages of flexible exchange rates, or even of the possibilities of monetary and fiscal control, but several points should be emphasised in view of a recent trend toward a 'more' flexible exchange-rate system. Most importantly, one should realise that in the fixed system a new instrument – the reserve – is created so that countries do not have to employ domestic policy instruments in order to deal with undesirable price effects from changes in exchange rates. There are still quantity effects, of course, and one of these involves the use of domestic monetary policy to try to offset changes in the monetary base which are induced by changes in the basic balance-of-payments situation. Under the perfectly flexible system the 'reserve' instrument is eliminated, and countries are tied together by both price and quantity effects; further, there will be monetary repercussions of shifts in both trade patterns and in capital movements. From this point of view, the fixed exchange-rate system is superior in creating a new instrument to introduce a measure of flexibility to domestic policy in this respect. But that is not all there is to it and, indeed, the story of the breakdown of the payments mechanism illustrates why one might, in the end, favour flexible rates, along with many economists of both a monetarist and non-monetarist stamp.

As the 1960s waned, many countries felt the pinch of the increasingly inadequate global reserves – in terms of more frequent uses of domestic policy instruments to deal with exchange problems – and a general softening of labour markets created a climate favourable to considering reform of the system. Numerous conferences were held, but the most we obtained was the very modest Special Drawing Right scheme [97]. In the meantime, non-random devaluations, becoming more and more obvious to speculators, were building up both an atmosphere of distrust of the system and its managers and a pool of volatile 'hot' money capable of undermining the system. The phenomenal growth of the Eurodollar market is a case in point. Looking back, it seems small wonder that the U.S. dollar deficits became increasingly greater if only because in this way countries obtained the necessary foreign exchange to enable them to stay on their fixed exchange rates. But the United States could not persist in this *ad hoc* way, nor could a world of countries faced with a massive exchange-induced build-up of domestic monetary bases, and so a period of limited flexibility ensued. In this present state, exchange rates are drifting about, while governments use their enlarged (and still growing) pool of dollar reserves to control the rate of change; it is under these circumstances that we must find a way to go.

From this point of view it is not hard to understand the

75

nature of the world-wide inflation, at least with respect to two of its causes [45]. That is to say, what we have seen is a general tendency toward rising unemployment, which has started up the fiscal and monetary machinery (directly, or to help in the financing of the fiscal policy), and towards increasing international liquidity, itself leading to generally larger monetary bases. Other causes abound, of course, but this is a book on monetary policy, so it is sufficient here to note that these 'exogenous' forces are at work, and are of sufficient volume to do the job. We note, somewhat parenthetically, that to the extent such forces are unpredictable – and presently the size of the budget deficit seems just as unpredictable as the basic payments situation – the use of the money stock (or its rate of change) as a policy target seems ill-advised. The case for money as an indicator, however, has not been weakened by the arguments presented here.

U.K. MONETARY POLICY SINCE 1951 [46, 54]

The main point of this discussion will be to consider the development of a policy announced in 1971 [10] which is now known as 'competition and credit control'. We begin the story in 1951 because that is the point at which U.K. monetary policy was partially freed from its war-time role of holding firm on the price of the debt of the U.K. government; the world-wide inflation caused by the Korean War, which saw upward pressure on money rates of interest, was the immediate cause of the abandonment of these pegging operations. From 1951 until the Radcliffe Committee reported in 1959 [89] U.K. monetary policy was tied up with the attempt to obtain full convertibility for sterling. Policy, even then, was 'stop–go', although it wasn't until the following period, 1959–71, that the term came to be widely used to describe the methods of the authorities. Basically, the system was brought up sharply by slamming on a variety of controls, whenever a balance-of-payments crisis appeared, as they did frequently after 1959.

The Radcliffe Committee probed deeply into the workings

of the monetary system and is still the standard source on many technical matters about the U.K. system. The Committee heard evidence to the following effect [46]:

(1) The authorities believed that their operations in long-term securities were necessary to that market because it was critical to the steady growth of the economy, to the prudent management of the public debt,[1] and to the appearance of the United Kingdom in the eyes of foreign investors and governments. The form this policy took was that of stabilising the market by 'leaning into the wind', whichever way it blew.

(2) In the Treasury-bill market, intermediaries known as 'discount houses' normally bid for the entire offering of Treasury bills. An amount will be allocated to them by the authorities, with the balance being taken up by the Bank of England. Commercial banks obtain their bills from the discount houses, as do other customers. The discount houses use commercial banks as the chief source of the funds they need to effect the purchase of Treasury bills in the first instance (on a 'call' basis). A policy of open-market operations would cause banks to call in funds from the discount houses which would then borrow from the Bank of England at Bank Rate. Bank Rate, changes in which were deliberately the subject of much publicity, was generally set at what was judged to be a 'penalty' figure. This policy was primarily directed at the control of interest rates, since the action of the discount houses in borrowing from the Bank of England essentially undid the original open-market operation, so far as changes in the quantity of money were concerned. It was felt that control of interest rates forced desirable domestic portfolio changes and, more importantly, tended to draw funds from foreign sources to help the balance of payments. The Radcliffe Committee was critical of this sort of policy and advocated a control over the entire stock of liquidity in the economy.

[1]One interest appears to have been in the 'funding' of the National Debt, a process whereby short-term securities were exchanged for long-term ones when conditions were right; 'liquidity' was also reduced in this way.

(3)   Since the authorities exerted little control over liquid assets by their policy of varying interest rates, they presumably were unable to affect the monetary base and therefore the money supply, however that entity might be defined.

The Radcliffe Committee was dubious of a policy of control of the money stock but, throughout the 1960s, the authorities seem gradually to have moved into a monetarist position. Mounting evidence of the stability of the demand for money [46], now perhaps not so readily accepted, as well as the increasing difficulty of their international position, seems to have forced this view [79]. Be that as it may, the new policy of 'competition and credit control' was announced in May 1971 [10] amid a furious debate (see especially [6]).

While in the brief retrospect that we have at our disposal this policy seems tame enough, in the context of what went before, some interesting changes have been made. The main departures, somewhat modified by even more recent experience, are:

(1)   During the 1960s, an increasing use of 'ceilings on advances', often effected by letters to the banks, was noted; Special Deposits from commercial banks were also often called to reinforce the government's general policy. These devices seemed to have a particularly strong impact on commercial banks, and the new policy promised less of this sort of control and more over the basic liquid assets of other financial intermediaries, including the discount houses. This part of the new policy seems very Radcliffean in its nature, but the purpose in 1971 was as much to introduce fairness and competition among intermediaries as to provide a more effective control over liquidity.

(2)   The authorities have abandoned the use of Bank Rate as such, in favour of continuous changes in their 'discount rate', since the former was judged to provide too much publicity to their activities. They also announced their intention of ceasing to support the market for long-term government securities. Partly, these changes were designed to free their hands to conduct a policy in monetary quantities, and partly to enable

them to discontinue their practice of supporting the cartel agreement on interest rates in the financial community (most notably among the commercial banks). This latter device was clearly designed to foster competition.

(3) While their expression of belief in the usefulness of simple monetarist prescriptions seems far from apostolic, they have announced a general switch from monitoring liquid assets or bank liabilities to monitoring one or the other of the monetary aggregates, M_1 (narrow money) or M_3 (narrow money plus a whole range of interest-bearing deposits in banks and financial intermediaries). Their operating target, to achieve this control, seems to be a broad measure of the monetary base, rather than a cash base. The broader base, which includes eligible commercial bills and call money on the London money market, has the significant disadvantage of not being determined by the authorities [6]; this, of course, is unsound, as noted in Chapter 3. Indeed, the authorities have been using controls over bank advances and other controls such as Special Deposits almost from the inception of the new policy, so their rationale should not be taken too literally.

To conclude, mention should be made of the international aspects of recent U.K. policy, particularly in view of the likelihood that the recent inflation has a partly international character. Indeed, international events have always been significant for the United Kingdom. It was concern with the return to convertibility which dominated the pre-Radcliffean policy, and there is little doubt that the periodic crises of the 1960s were caused by an overvalued currency [94]. Finally, in the new era after 1971, while not much has been made of it in official documents, we have seen another monetarist favourite, that of the fluctuating exchange rate, in use in the United Kingdom and elsewhere.

MONETARY POLICY IN THE UNITED STATES AFTER 1951 [68]

In the United States, as in the United Kingdom, the monetary authorities were freed from their role of stabilising the price of debt in 1951; in this case an almost formal declaration, subsequently known as the Accord, was promulgated. Again, one can distinguish several sub-periods in the years that have followed, although in the U.S. case the dating is not based primarily on changes in the operating techniques of the central bank.

During the early years until 1958, most of which had Eisenhower in the White House, monetary policy was essentially passive, and Keynesian methods of control were considered adequate. In fact, it is more likely that the United States was in some kind of delicate balance than that fiscal policy was really working, but whatever one might think of those buoyant years the system showed signs of strain after 1958. In particular, one noticed a balance-of-payments problem, a slower rate of growth, and the first appearance of 'stagflation' a condition which had been expected to appear some ten years earlier. In those difficult times, until 1968 at least, there were four central aspects to the Federal Reserve's operating procedures.

(1) They believed that the ideal way to conduct open-market operations was in Treasury Bills. The reason for this 'bills-only' policy varied [29, 91, 113], but prominent was the feeling that operations in long-term securities, where markets were judged to be especially thin, would upset potentially unstable capital markets and unleash the cycle in the form of an investment 'multiplier–accelerator' reaction. There was also a general feeling that all interest rates tended to move together anyway, because of the influence of expectations.[1]

[1]These ideas are not entirely consistent. Just about the time that the latter view got a firm boost in the work of David Meiselman [70], the authorities abandoned the policy. There was a flirtation with something called 'operation twist' during the period. The idea

This policy dominated the first ten years of the post-Accord period.

(2) In order to guide their policy, the Federal Reserve put its faith in a 'free-reserves' (excess reserves less borrowed reserves) operating target. But a rise of free reserves can come about for a variety of reasons, some of which would not imply that money markets have eased [69], and the authorities, in the face of a persistent academic criticism of their procedure, gradually moved towards a stance of looking at other monetary quantities, the volume of bank lending, as well as free reserves. This multiplicity of targets, while not necessarily undesirable in a completely articulated policy model, leaves one a little uneasy in that the interactions between the targets, and the nature of the indicators, are not spelled out precisely.

(3) Throughout, in the face of severe criticism, the authorities have clung to an imprecise collection of monetary indicators now known as the 'tone and feel' of the market [7, 47]. This is still the case to a certain extent, and the disadvantages of an imprecise measure, the meaning of which not all policy-makers would agree on, has to be weighed against the 'advantage' of secrecy and, to be sure, of relying on the expertise of the monetary authorities in this direct way. Of course, in the present climate, where the clamour for results is especially great, it is not surprising that 'tone and feel' would survive, since its vagueness forms a protective shield for the embattled monetary authorities.

(4) Finally, as an undercurrent rather than as an announced policy, one must note that there has been some official accep-

---

was to force up short-term rates, to attract funds from foreign centres and force down, or maintain, long-term rates, to aid the rate of growth, thus 'twisting' the yield curve away from its usual upward slope. If, however, long-term rates are simple averages of future expected short-term rates, and if expectations about what is going to happen to short-term rates depends only on the behaviour of short-term rates in recent months, it would be difficult to actually effect the 'twist'. Thus interest rates might be expected to move together, at least broadly.

tance of the idea that the principal intermediate effect of monetary policy was not on the quantity of money (as such) or the interest rate, but on the 'availability of loanable funds'. This idea relies on imperfections and discrimination in lending practices, with the result that any exact link between the monetary base and final spending is broken [57]. It pushes one in the direction of considering a variety of targets and indicators, even of a subjective nature.

What is new about policy in recent years is that, in fits and starts, the monetary mechanism, alternating or working jointly with 'incomes' policies of various degrees of firmness, has been employed. We have even seen some periods in which the money stock has been held constant, but the 'stop–go' nature of the controls has been such that the average rate of growth of the money stock has been quite high, relative to what might have been desirable, judged with hindsight. The failure of these half-hearted attempts has tended to put the monetarist prescriptions into a bad light and, one suspects, monetarism is once again on the wane in the United States [72]. This seems certain to suggest a painful adjustment to ease the present problem of stagflation [72, 44].

Bibliography

[1] S. Almon, 'The Distributed Lag Between Capital Appropriations and Expenditures', *Econometrica* (Jan 1965).

[2] L. C. Andersen and J. L. Jordan, 'Monetary and Fiscal Actions: A Test of Their Relative Importance in Economic Stabilization', *Federal Reserve Bank of St Louis Review* (Nov 1968).

[3] A. Ando and F. Modigliani, 'The Relative Stability of Monetary Velocity and the Investment Multiplier', *American Economic Review* (Sep 1965).

[4] V. Argy, 'The Impact of Monetary Policy on Expenditure, With Particular Reference to the United Kingdom', *I.M.F. Staff Papers* (Nov 1969).

[5] V. Argy, 'The Role of Money in Economic Activity: Some Results for 17 Developed Countries', *I.M.F. Staff Papers* (Nov 1970).

[6] M. Artis and J. M. Parkin, 'A General Appraisal', [of 'competition and credit control'] *Bankers Magazine* (1971).

[7] T. R. Atkinson, 'Tone and Feel of the Market as a Guide for Federal Open Market Operations', in *Targets and Indicators of Monetary Policy*, ed. K. Brunner (San Francisco: Chandler, 1969).

[8] M. J. Bailey, *National Income and the Price Level* (New York: McGraw–Hill, 1962).

[9] R. J. Ball, *Inflation and the Theory of Money* (London: Allen & Unwin, 1964).

[10] Bank of England, 'Competition and Credit Control', articles from the *Quarterly Bulletin*, vol. 11 (1971).

[11] C. R. Barrett and A. A. Walters, 'The Relative Stability

of Monetary and Autonomous Expenditures Multipliers in the U.K.', *Review of Economics and Statistics* (Nov 1966).

[12] N. Bowsher and L. Kalish, 'Does Slower Monetary Expansion Discriminate Against Housing?', *Federal Reserve Bank of St Louis Review* (June 1968).

[13] M. Bronfenbrenner, *Income Distribution Theory* (Chicago: Aldine-Atherton, 1971).

[14] K. Brunner and A. H. Meltzer, 'The Meaning of Monetary Indicators', in *Monetary Process and Policy*, ed. G. Horwich (Homewood, Ill.: Irwin, 1967).

[15] K. Brunner, *Targets and Indicators of Monetary Policy* (San Francisco: Chandler, 1969).

[16] K. Brunner and A. H. Meltzer, 'The Nature of the Policy Problem', in *Targets and Indicators of Monetary Policy*, ed. K. Brunner (San Francisco: Chandler, 1969).

[17] P. Cagan, *Determinants and Effects of Changes in the Stock of Money, 1875–1960* (New York: Columbia University Press, 1965).

[18] P. Cagan, 'The Monetary Dynamics of Hyper-Inflation', in *Studies in the Quantity Theory of Money*, ed. M. Friedman (University of Chicago Press, 1956).

[19] P. Cagan, 'Theories of Mild, Continuing Inflation', in *Inflation: Its Causes, Consequences, and Control*, ed. S. W. Rousseas (Wilton, Conn.: Kazanjian Foundation, 1969).

[20] V. Chick, *The Theory of Monetary Policy* (London: Gray-Mills, 1973).

[21] C. Christ, 'Monetary and Fiscal Influences on U.S. Money Income, 1891–1970', *Journal of Money, Credit and Banking* (Feb 1973).

[22] J. W. Christian, 'A Further Analysis of the Objectives of American Monetary Policy', *Journal of Finance* (June 1968).

[23] Commission on Money and Credit, *Money and Credit* (Englewood Cliffs, N.J.: Prentice-Hall, 1961).

[24] A. S. Courakis, 'Monetary Policy: Old Wisdom Behind a New Façade', *Economica* (Feb 1973).

[25] J. R. Crotty, 'Specification Error in Macro-Econometric Models: The Influence of Policy Goals', *American Economic Review* (Dec 1973).

[26] P. Davidson and S. Weintraub, 'Money as Cause and Effect', *Economic Journal* (Dec 1973).

[27] M. DePrano and T. Mayer, 'Tests of the Relative Importance of Autonomous Expenditures and Money', *American Economic Review* (Sep 1965).

[28] W. G. Dewald and H. G. Johnson, 'An Objective Analysis of the Objectives of American Monetary Policy, 1952–61', in *Banking and Monetary Studies*, ed. D. Carson (Homewood, Ill.: Irwin, 1963).

[29] D. I. Fand, 'A Time Series Analysis of the "Bills Only" Theory of Interest Rates', *Review of Economics and Statistics* (Nov 1966).

[30] Federal Reserve Bank of Boston, *Consumer Spending and Monetary Policy: The Linkages* (1971).

[31] S. Fischer and J. P. Cooper, 'Stabilization Policy and Lags', *Journal of Political Economy* (July–Aug 1973).

[32] D. Fisher 'The Objectives of British Monetary Policy, 1951–64', *Journal of Finance* (Dec 1968).

[33] D. Fisher, 'The Instruments of Monetary Policy and the Generalised Trade-Off Function for Britain, 1955–1968', *Manchester School* (Sep 1970).

[34] D. Fisher, 'Targets and Indicators of British Monetary Policy', *Bankers Magazine* (Sep 1973).

[35] G. Fisher and D. Sheppard, *Effects of Monetary Policy on the United States Economy: A Survey of Econometric Evidence*, O.E.C.D. Economic Outlook, Occasional Studies (Paris: O.E.C.D., Dec 1972).

[36] E. Foster, 'Costs and Benefits of Inflation', *Studies in Monetary Economics* (Federal Reserve Bank of Minneapolis, 1972).

[37] M. Friedman and A. J. Schwartz, *A Monetary History of the United States, 1867–1960* (New York: Columbia University Press, 1963).

[38] M. Friedman and W. W. Heller, *Monetary Vs. Fiscal Policy* (New York: Norton, 1969).

[39]   M. Friedman and A. J. Schwartz, *Monetary Statistics of the United States* (New York: Columbia University Press, 1970).

[40]   M. Friedman, 'The Monetary Studies of the National Bureau', in M. Friedman, *Studies in the Optimum Quantity of Money* (Chicago: Aldine, 1969).

[41]   M. Friedman, 'A Monetary Theory of Nominal Income', *Journal of Political Economy* (Mar–Apr 1971).

[42]   M. Friedman, *A Program for Monetary Stability* (New York: Fordham University Press, 1960).

[43]   M. Friedman and D. Meiselman, 'The Relative Stability of Monetary Velocity and the Investment Multiplier in the United States, 1897–1958', in E. C. Brown, *et al.*, *Stabilization Policies* (Englewood Cliffs, N.J.: Prentice-Hall, 1963).

[44]   M. Friedman, 'The Role of Monetary Policy', *American Economic Review* (Mar 1968).

[45]   H. N. Goldstein, 'Monetary Policy Under Fixed and Floating Exchange Rates', *National Westminster Bank Quarterly Review* (Nov 1974).

[46]   C. A. E. Goodhart, 'Monetary Policy in the United Kingdom', in *Monetary Policy in Twelve Industrial Countries*, ed. K. Holbik (Federal Reserve Bank of Boston, 1973).

[47]   J. Guttentag, 'The Strategy of Open Market Operations', *Quarterly Journal of Economics* (Feb 1966).

[48]   M. Hamburger, 'Indicators of Monetary Policy: The Arguments and the Evidence', *American Economic Review* (May 1970).

[49]   B. Hansen, 'On the Effects of Fiscal and Monetary Policy: A Taxonomic Discussion', *American Economic Review* (Sep 1973).

[50]   H. H. Helbing and J. E. Turley, 'A Primer on Inflation: Its Conception, Its Costs, Its Consequences', *Federal Reserve Bank of St Louis Review* (Jan 1975).

[51]   P. Hendershott, *The Neutralised Money Stock* (Homewood, Ill.: Irwin, 1968).

[52]   P. Hendershott, 'The Full-Employment Interest Rate

and the Neutralized Money Stock: Comment', *Journal of Finance* (Mar 1971).

[53] J. R. Hicks, *Value and Capital*, 2nd edn (Oxford: Clarendon Press, 1946).

[54] K. Holbik (ed.), *Monetary Policy in Twelve Industrial Countries* (Federal Reserve Bank of Boston, 1973).

[55] E. P. Howrey, 'Distributed Lags and the Effectiveness of Monetary Policy', *American Economic Review* (Dec 1969).

[56] E. P. Howrey, 'Structural Change and Postwar Economic Stability: An Econometric Test', *Review of Economics and Statistics* (Feb 1970).

[57] D. Jaffee, *Credit Rationing and the Commercial Loan Market* (New York: Wiley, 1971).

[58] H. G. Johnson (ed.), *Readings in British Monetary Economics* (Oxford University Press, 1972).

[59] J. Johnston, *Econometric Methods*, 2nd edn (New York: McGraw-Hill, 1972).

[60] N. Kaldor (ed.), *Conflicts Among Policy Objectives* (Oxford: Blackwell, 1971).

[61] M. W. Keran, 'Selecting a Monetary Indicator – Evidence From the United States and Other Developed Countries', *Federal Reserve Bank of St Louis Review* (Sep 1970).

[62] A. O. Krueger, 'The Impact of Alternative Government Policies Under Varying Exchange Systems', *Quarterly Journal of Economics* (May 1965).

[63] R. E. Knight, 'Reserve Requirements', *Federal Reserve Bank of Kansas City Monthly Review* (Apr–May 1974).

[64] D. Laidler, 'The Permanent Income Concept in a Macro-Economic Model', *Oxford Economic Papers* (Mar 1968).

[65] D. Laidler, 'The Influence of Money on Real Income and Inflation – A Simple Model with Some Empirical Tests for the United States, 1953–72', *Manchester School* (Dec 1973).

[66] F. de Leeuw and J. Kalchbrenner, 'Monetary and Fiscal Actions: A Test of Their Relative Importance

in Economic Stabilization – Comment', *Federal Reserve Bank of St Louis Review* (Apr 1969).

[67] A. Leijonhufvud, *On Keynesian Economics and the Economics of Keynes* (Oxford University Press, 1968).

[68] T. Mayer, *Monetary Policy in the United States* (New York: Random House, 1968).

[69] A. J. Meigs, *Free Reserves and the Money Supply* (University of Chicago Press, 1962).

[70] D. Meiselman, *The Term Structure of Interest Rates* (Englewood Cliffs, N.J.: Prentice-Hall, 1962).

[71] D. Meiselman (ed.), *Varieties of Monetary Experience* (University of Chicago Press, 1971).

[72] D. Meiselman, 'The 1973 Report of the President's Council of Economic Advisors: Whistling in the Dark', *American Economic Review* (Sep 1973).

[73] A. H. Meltzer, 'Public Policies as Causes of Fluctuations', *Journal of Money, Credit and Banking* (Feb 1970).

[74] F. Modigliani, 'Monetary Policy and Consumption', in *Consumer Spending and Monetary Policy: The Linkages* (Federal Reserve Bank of Boston, 1971).

[75] B. J. Moore, 'Optimal Monetary Policy', *Economic Journal* (Mar 1972).

[76] R. A. Mundell, *Monetary Theory* (Pacific Palisades, California: Goodyear, 1971).

[77] R. A. Mundell, 'The Monetary Dynamics of International Adjustment Under Fixed and Flexible Exchange Rates', *Quarterly Journal of Economics* (May 1960).

[78] W. T. Newlyn, 'The Supply of Money and Its Control', *Economic Journal* (June 1964).

[79] A. R. Nobay, 'The Bank of England, Monetary Policy and Monetary Theory in the United Kingdom, 1951–1971', *Manchester School* (Mar 1973).

[80] J. M. O'Brien, 'Federal Regulation of Stock Market Credit: A Need for Reconsideration', *Federal Reserve Bank of Philadelphia Business Review* (July–Aug 1974).

[81] A. F. Ott and D. J. Ott, 'Monetary and Fiscal Policy: Goals and the Choice of Instruments', *Quarterly Journal of Economics* (May 1968).

[82] Y. C. Park, 'Some Current Issues on the Transmission Process of Monetary Policy', *I.M.F. Staff Papers* (Mar 1972).

[83] D. Patinkin, *Money, Interest and Prices*, 2nd edn (New York: Harper & Row, 1965).

[84] B. P. Pesek and T. R. Saving, *Money, Wealth and Economic Theory* (New York: Macmillan, 1967).

[85] M. H. Peston, *Theory of Macroeconomic Policy* (Oxford: Philip Allan, 1974).

[86] C. Pissarides, 'A Model of British Macro-Economic Policy, 1955–1969', *Manchester School* (Sep 1972).

[87] W. Poole, 'Optimal Choice of Monetary Policy Instruments in a Simple Stochastic Macro Model', *Quarterly Journal of Economics* (May 1970).

[88] W. Poole and E. B. F. Kornbluth, 'The Friedman–Meiselman CMC Paper: New Evidence on an Old Controversy', *American Economic Review* (Dec 1973).

[89] *Report of the Committee on the Working of the Monetary System*, Cmnd. 827 (London: H.M.S.O., Aug 1959).

[90] G. L. Reuber, 'The Objectives of Canadian Monetary Policy, 1949–61: Empirical "Trade-Offs" and the Reaction Function of the Authorities', *Journal of Political Economy* (Apr 1964).

[91] W. W. Riefler, 'Open Market Operations in Long-Term Securities', *Federal Reserve Bulletin* (Nov 1958).

[92] L. Ritter, 'Official Central Banking Theory in the United States, 1939–61', *Journal of Political Economy* (Feb 1962).

[93] M. H. Ross, 'Operation Twist: A Mistaken Policy?' *Journal of Political Economy* (Aug 1967).

[94] D. C. Rowan, 'The Monetary System in the Fifties and Sixties', *Manchester School* (Mar 1973).

[95] T. Saving, 'Monetary-Policy Targets and Indicators', *Journal of Political Economy* (Aug 1967).

[96] T. Saving, 'Outside Money, Inside Money, and the Real Balance Effect', *Journal of Money, Credit and Banking* (Feb 1970).

[97] W. M. Scammel, *International Trade and Payments* (New York: St Martin's Press, 1974).

[98] A. J. Schwartz, 'Short Term Targets of Three Foreign Central Banks', in *Targets and Indicators of Monetary Policy*, ed. K. Brunner (San Francisco: Chandler, 1969).

[99] J. L. Scadding, 'The Fiscal Element in Monetary Policy: 1965–8', *Journal of Money, Credit and Banking* (May 1971).

[100] W. L. Smith, 'Financial Intermediaries and Monetary Control', *Journal of Finance* (May 1959).

[101] E. Sohmen, 'Fiscal and Monetary Policies under Alternative Exchange Rate Systems', *Quarterly Journal of Economics* (Aug 1967).

[102] R. W. Spencer, 'Channels of Monetary Influence: A Survey', *Federal Reserve Bank of St Louis Review* (Nov 1974).

[103] D. Starleaf and J. Stephenson, 'A Suggested Solution to the Monetary Indicator Problem: The Monetary Full Employment Interest Rate', *Journal of Finance* (Sep 1969).

[104] J. L. Stein, 'A Method of Identifying Disturbances Which Produce Changes in Money National Income', *Journal of Political Economy* (Feb 1960).

[105] J. E. Tanner, 'Indicators of Monetary Policy: An Evaluation of Five', *Banca Nazionale del Lavoro Quarterly Review* (Dec 1972).

[106] J. Tobin, 'Money and Income: Post Hoc Ergo Propter Hoc?' *Quarterly Journal of Economics* (May 1970).

[107] J. Tobin, 'Inflation and Unemployment', *American Economic Review* (Mar 1972).

[108] D. P. Tucker, 'Dynamic Income Adjustments to Money Supply Changes', *American Economic Review* (June 1966).

[109] D. P. Villanueva, 'Statistical Analysis of Discount Rate Policy in Belgium, 1957–1968', *European Economic Review* (1972).

[110] A. A. Walters, 'Monetary Multipliers in the U.K., 1880–1962', *Oxford Economic Papers* (Nov 1966).

[111] J. Williamson, 'International Liquidity', *Economic Journal* (Sep 1973).

[112] J. H. Wood, 'A Model of Federal Reserve Behavior', in *Monetary Process and Policy*, ed. G. Horwich (Homewood, Ill.: Irwin, 1967).

[113] R. A. Young and C. A. Yager, 'The Economics of "Bills Preferably" ', *Quarterly Journal of Economics* (Aug 1960).

[114] R. Zecher, 'Implications of Four Econometric Models for the Indicators Issue', *American Economic Review* (May 1970).